DOMESDAY BOOK

ITS PLACE IN ADMINISTRATIVE HISTORY

BY

V. H. GALBRAITH

OXFORD
AT THE CLARENDON PRESS
1974

Oxford University Press, Ely House, London W.1

GLASGOW NEW YORK TORONTO MELBOURNE WELLINGTON
CAPE TOWN IBADAN NAIROBI DAR ES SALAAM LUSAKA ADDIS ABABA
DELHI BOMBAY CALCUTTA MADRAS KARACHI LAHORE DACCA
KUALA LUMPUR SINGAPORE HONG KONG TOKYO

ISBN 0 19 822424 9

*Printed in Great Britain
at the University Press, Oxford
by Vivian Ridler
Printer to the University*

TO G. R. G.

PREFACE

THIS book assumes the main conclusions reached in *The Making of Domesday Book* (Clarendon Press, 1961). In that volume I criticized the obsession of Victorian scholars with the Anglo-Saxon geld and the false assumption that the returns to the Domesday Inquest were a vast collection of Hundred Rolls.

In this book I am concerned with the basic importance of Domesday Book in later English administrative history. The book was completed nearly two years ago with the valuable help of Mrs. Olive Smith, but its publication has been delayed owing to circumstances beyond my control. It is inscribed, like its predecessor, to my wife, my best critic, on whom has also fallen the whole drudgery involved in its publication.

V. H. G.

The frontispiece was paid for from the sum given to V. H. G. on his eightieth birthday by his friends and pupils.

CONTENTS

INTRODUCTION

LOOKING backwards, the half-century preceding the Great War of 1914 stands out as the golden age of the writing of history in England; and in no branch of the subject is this truer than in Domesday studies. The researches of Maitland, Round, and other scholars of near-genius combined to penetrate the secrets of this unique, yet baffling, factual record, and their conclusions, though hotly disputed in their lifetimes, have since won such general acceptance that today their fame has become almost legendary. The meaning of the great Survey cannot be approached, much less mastered, without some preliminary study of *Domesday Book and Beyond* (1897) and *Feudal England* (1895). Indeed, so great has been their impact that in recent years the main interest of eleventh-century historians has turned increasingly from constitutional and legal history to biography and social history. This study of persons and of peoples has entailed a new and sustained research into the scanty literary sources and peripheral evidence such as the Bayeux tapestry and the coronation services; and a series of elaborate lives of our early kings seems likely to alter radically hitherto accepted views. A single instance will here suffice to illustrate this shift of interest. Every schoolboy knows that the enigmatic personality of Edward the Confessor broods over each page of Domesday Book which records for every estate the name of its owner 'on the day when King Edward was alive and dead'. Maitland described him as follows:

Had Canute's successors been his equals in vigour and wisdom, perhaps the change [of the whole economic and political structure] might have been consummated peacefully, and by means of written laws which we now might be reading. As it was, there came to the throne the holy but imbecile Edward. In after days he won not only the halo of the saint, to which he may have been entitled, but the fame, to which he was certainly not entitled, of having been a great legislator. In the minster that he reared, king after king made oath to observe the laws of the Confessor. So far as we know he never made a law. Had he made laws, had he even made good use of those that were already made, there might have been no Norman Conquest of England. But then, had there been no Norman Conquest of England, Edward would never have gained his fictitious glories. As it was, men looked back to him as the last of the English kings of the English—for of Harold, who had become the perjured usurper, there could be no talk—and galled by the yoke of their French masters, they sighed for St. Edward's law, meaning thereby the law that had prevailed in a yet unvanquished England.[1]

This verdict, with which few would have disagreed in 1893 when Maitland wrote, is wholly irreconcilable with Professor Barlow's[2] recent portrait of a king who controlled events for twenty-four years and left behind him a united kingdom.

This 'cult of personality'—a world-wide phenomenon today—affords to our contemporary writers a greater freedom of interpretation and imaginative reconstruction than ever before, and, when applied in so early a period, assigns to the pitifully inadequate monastic chronicles an authority of testimony which is itself something of an anachronism. Certainly, it would not have passed muster in Maitland's lifetime, as Edward Augustus Freeman, its chief Victorian exponent, found to his cost. But, at least, it reminds us that medieval scholarship is pursued today in a climate of opinion totally different from that of the nineteenth century. In every country the historical masterpieces then produced were inspired not by any love of research for its own sake, but by the practical problem of explaining the origins of the liberal struggles towards 'free' governments all over Europe. In this movement, scholars relied overwhelmingly on the printed

[1] *Collected Papers* (1911), vol. ii, p. 423.
[2] *Edward the Confessor* (1970).

word, leaving the study of manuscripts to librarians and to the civil servants of the British Museum and the Public Record Office. Maitland himself was outstanding in his generation as a historian who could at least read them with accuracy. Yet even he praised T. F. Tout for having 'discovered' two large rolls in the Record Office and for having then grappled with 'this promising yet repulsive material.'[1] Today—seventy years later—the study of the past in England has caught up with that of the Continent, in the process becoming less slanted, less political, and much more academic. Its devotees have come to enjoy the very process of research upon manuscripts, and can fairly claim to approach their problems with greater single-mindedness than their Victorian predecessors.

Improved technique, however, has given rise to new problems, and historians are more highly specialized than ever before. Maitland is remembered as the historian of law in England. In the *History of English Law* (1895) and *Domesday Book and Beyond* (1897) he surveyed its growth from the earliest times to the reign of Edward I, a period that is of close upon a thousand years, including within his survey an examination of the origins of town life, the development of farming and agriculture, the Church, feudalism, and even of Diplomatic. Today no such breadth of treatment is possible, owing to the emergence of Economic, Agricultural, and Municipal History, each a separate field of inquiry in its own right. Maitland's correspondence[2] shows him casting a wide net in his search for expert guidance through the many centuries which preceded the rise of the Common Law. Even so, he had to take much for granted; and in particular he relied too much upon both J. H. Round and Vinogradoff, with unfortunate results. From Round he took over his

[1] *Collected Papers*, vol. iii, p. 490, from a review of *State Trials of the Reign of Edward I* (1906), to which he appended a full page of MSS. corrigenda.
[2] *The Letters of Frederic William Maitland*, ed. C. H. S. Fifoot (1965). Among the younger scholars who helped him were Adolphus Ballard, W. J. Corbett, W. H. Stevenson, Mary Bateson, G. J. Turner, and James Tait.

too hasty and too dogmatic explanation of the compilation of Domesday Book; and from Vinogradoff much unsubstantiated theorizing regarding the 'stock of freedom' surviving in England from the Anglo-Saxon conquest. These were no small matters, and time has dealt hardly with both. As a result, modern readers are faced with the dilemma that the two most illuminating works extant on early English society are shot through with these borrowed assumptions, which still mar more recent work.

The final and obvious factor in the changed climate of thought regarding the remote past lies, quite simply, in the mere lapse of time. In the nineteenth century, historical research was the private hobby of a few, mainly well-to-do people: today it has become a heavily subsidized activity, professionally followed by hundreds of specialized scholars. Their contributions, together with the mounting publications of the Public Record Office, the British Museum, the Royal Historical Society, and many local history bodies, have increased our knowledge, and at the same time laid new bibliographical problems on the shoulders of research historians both in Europe and in America. All this activity can be confidently expected to enlarge and alter our knowledge; but today the solid basis of Domesday studies is still the works of the Victorians, and that it should be so is the true measure of their greatness.

These reflections suggest that the social assumptions of Victorian historians are no longer relevant; and so, that contemporary thinking calls for a restatement of Domesday problems. But today, more than the mere lapse of time is at stake. The whole hypothesis then accepted regarding the Survey is now no longer tenable. The motives the Victorians put forward for its compilation and for the process of making it, and for its later importance in English history are more than inadequate. They are flatly incorrect. Broadly speaking, nineteenth-century research still stands foursquare so far as it has been used to rewrite the general history of the period, and is still the best introduction to later work published in the *Victoria County History*, in the Royal Historical and local society transactions as well as in our standard textbooks. Yet, as a contribution to administrative history it can only mislead us; and this is the more serious in that Domesday Book is the first, large *written* record produced in a European society that was, for the most part, still both local and oral. No satisfactory precedent for its compilation is known. Contrariwise, Domesday itself formed a precedent widely followed later, not only in England but all over Europe. It is in short a revolutionary, forward-looking document, carried out in an age of rapid development in every branch of civilized life, both ecclesiastical and lay. Considered in this light, the error of our classic Victorian authors is threefold.

First, as regards its purpose, they all agreed that it was a purely fact-finding survey, designed to make possible a new and more just reassessment of the ancient geld or Danegeld. The credit for this discovery (as it seemed to them) was due to J. H. Round; but, in fact, it is a deep-seated anachronism, whose origins lie behind either Round (or Freeman), behind even Ellis's *General Introduction to Domesday* (1833).[1] It is supported by no shred of hard evidence. Even so, the error still persists in most of our standard histories, and is examined below in some detail.

Secondly, the Victorians gravely misunderstood the actual administrative process by which the Survey was carried out. Without exception they failed to profit from the near-miracle by which the actual original manuscripts written in 1086 and 1087 are still preserved, preferring to work from the printed version. These manuscripts still hold secrets, to be won in the future by scholars better technically equipped to deal with the problems of Palaeography and Diplomatic. But already it has become incredible that the 'original returns' made by the separate

[1] See Chapter XI, below.

circuits of inquirers were geographically arranged as 'Hundred Rolls', which were then discarded at Winchester in favour of Domesday Book as we have it, that is, a statement of royal demesne, followed by the detailed honours of each tenant-in-chief, arranged county by county. The fallacy of the Victorian view is worked out in detail in *The Making of Domesday Book* (1961).

Thirdly, the Victorian masters, arguing backwards from the known to the unknown, ignored the paramount influence exercised by Domesday Book on later English administrative development. This neglect has continued since, thanks to Maitland's *Domesday Book and Beyond*, in which the Survey was used to pierce the obscurity of Anglo-Saxon history. It may be doubted whether any great writer, except perhaps Stubbs, has fully realized the creative force which underlay the measures taken by all medieval governments in the high Middle Ages. Though always appealing to the past they were consciously building a new kind of state which, in retrospect, was—long afterwards—labelled Feudalism. It was an aristocratic structure based upon the exploitation of royal power by sovereign kings whose absolutism was first fostered by the Catholic Church. Domesday Book was, in fact, a blue print of the new order introduced by William I. Within a century of its compilation, the society described in it was transformed by the development of the Common Law and the centralization of justice and taxation. The geld and other county renders gave way to the organization of knights' fees, and royal control was replaced by the growth of the Chancery and the Exchequer, each step in the process requiring reference back to the Survey. The persistence of its original authority through more than three centuries of history is reflected in the title I have ventured to give to this book. Such a conclusion is borne out by all that Maitland wrote, though the immediate purpose of his Domesday studies was to explain the origins of the profound differences between

the Old English and the continental systems. The rapid
growth of Administrative History after his death owes
much to the *History of English Law*, to which it has added
the close study of the royal household and its officers,
and of government by seals and writs, which superseded
the oral and customary society of earlier centuries.

The criticisms of our standard Domesday authorities,
however crudely summarized above, are no more than
necessary deductions drawn from the study of Administrative History. The rise of this approach to the past was
long delayed in England by the national obsession with
the origins of our unique parliamentary system of government; and it is no accident that the researches of T. F.
Tout (1855–1929), its chief exponent, were sparked off
by reviewing a study[1] of French administrative history in
the late thirteenth and fourteenth centuries. The findings
of his six-volume *Chapters in the Administrative History of
Mediaeval England*, published during the last ten years of
his life, were not so revolutionary as he had hoped at the
outset; yet they had the vital effect of focusing attention on
the king's household from the earliest times for which
written evidence survives, to wit, the end of the tenth
century. This late start explains the neglect of administrative history by the Victorians, intent upon proving the
survival of a free German peasantry from the Anglo-
Saxon conquest five centuries earlier.

'If once', wrote Maitland in 1888,[2] 'we were certain
of our twelfth century we might understand Domesday,
if once we understood the state of England on the day
when the Confessor was alive and dead, then we might

---

[1] Eugene Déprez, *Études de Diplomatique anglaise 1272–1485: le sceau privé; le
sceau secret; le signet* (Paris, 1908). Tout's review is in the *E.H.R.* 1908, pp. 556–9.
See T. F. Tout, *The Place of the Reign of Edward II in English History* (1914),
p. vi.

[2] *Collected Papers*, vol. i, p. 482. Cf. *Domesday Book and Beyond*, p. 356,
where he insists we can best avoid anachronisms by 'reading our history backwards as well as forwards, of making sure of our middle ages before we talk
about the "archaic", of accustoming our eyes to the twilight before we go out into
the night'.

turn with new hopes of success to the Anglo-Saxon dooms and land-books.' Such were the motives that inspired his *Domesday Book and Beyond* (1897), in which, though he wrote brilliantly of 'the dooms and land-books', his real subject was the 'fundamental controversies' regarding the free or unfree origins of English society.[1] The time may come—who knows?—when historians can 'go out into the night' of the age of settlement. But this moment is little, if any, nearer than in Maitland's lifetime; and the best minds[2] today, looking forwards instead of backwards, tend more and more to confine their researches to the only hard evidence available, that is, to Domesday Book itself. To me, at least, this new approach promises more sure results than the rash speculations of the nineteenth century regarding half a millennium which is, administratively speaking, virtually unrecorded.

The historians of royal administration have, since Maitland's day, traced the enduring influence which the Survey exerted upon the development of the royal curia in the twelfth and thirteenth centuries. Its evidence is firmly based upon the spoken word, either of juries or of individuals. But already *seisin* is often claimed on the written evidence of royal charters and sealed writs. The Survey's future importance lay simply in the fact that it put into writing for the first time a detailed statement of all the facts regarding a society still predominantly customary and oral. In the following century the royal administration depended more and more upon documents, culminating by the thirteenth century in a full-blown bureaucratic state—a complex of household departments, each issuing its own records under its own seal. There was much over-lapping, as each department became a vested interest, and the administration became bogged down in its pro-

---

[1] Its purpose is clearly stated on p. 221, at the beginning of Essay II, and the argument is continued in Essay III, on 'the Hide'.

[2] For example, R. Hoyt. See Chapter VIII, below.

cedures and precedents. But this complicated and hap-
hazard machine was the end-product of a state of affairs
first clearly defined in Domesday Book.

In this faith, I have collected the results of a lifetime's
study of Domesday Book and the administrative arrangements to which it later gave rise. It is not intended as a
book for beginners: rather, it is a book of reference for
those at pains to advance our knowledge by further study.
For this reason I have felt impelled to refer again and
again in successive chapters to the mistaken assumptions
which repeatedly mar the arguments of the Victorians. If
I have, thus, underlined their errors, it is simply because
Maitland and Round still remain the best sources for
the understanding of Domesday Book. Domesday Book
seeks only to put first things first, for until we are clear as
to why it was made, and how, we cannot hope to do justice
to its brooding presence through the administrative
developments of the three following centuries. No one, so
far as I am aware, has made any serious attempt to follow
the fortunes of Domesday Book during the late Middle
Ages, and they call for a much closer examination, pending
the appearance of a full-scale history of the English public
records.

The book makes no claim to supplement, much less to
rewrite, the straight narrative of William I's reign.
Nevertheless, when it was all but completed, I found myself so much at odds with recent writers that I have
ventured to add a few pages[1] at the end on wider issues.
The main question concerns the reign of King Harold,
and William's pretensions to succeed to the English
throne, before and after the battle of Hastings. These
matters are strictly relevant to Domesday Book, and
compel its historian to question the high place recently
assigned to the Bayeux tapestry as evidence of the sup-
positititious results of Harold's visit to France at some
unknown date before the death of Edward the Confessor.

[1] Below, pp. 173–83.

SELECT BIBLIOGRAPHY

T HE bibliography presents insuperable difficulties. I have tried in this volume to stick closely to the fortunes of Domesday Book itself across the ages; but these are inseparably bound up with the rapid developments of the royal administration. Of this expansion it was the conscious and deliberate *fons et origo*, and the text of the Survey is meaningless without some grasp of the king's household and the precocious extension of government by sealed writs and charters. The works cited below are therefore no more than an arbitrary and sparing selection of such as have proved of most assistance to me over half a century.

DOMESDAY BOOK

In 2 vols., preserved in the Public Record Office, Chancery Lane. The two volumes of Domesday Book were first published in consequence of an address by the House of Lords to King George III in 1767. The actual printing was not, however, commenced until 1773, and was completed in 1783.

Volume I or Great Domesday contains the Survey of the counties of Kent, Sussex, Surrey, Hampshire, Berkshire, Wiltshire, Dorset, Somerset, Devonshire, Cornwall, Middlesex, Hertfordshire, Buckinghamshire, Oxfordshire, Gloucestershire, Worcestershire, Herefordshire, Cambridgeshire, Huntingdonshire, Bedfordshire, Northamptonshire, Leicestershire, Warwickshire, Staffordshire, Shropshire, Cheshire, Derbyshire, Nottinghamshire, Yorkshire, and Lincolnshire.

Volume II or Little Domesday contains the Survey of Essex, Norfolk, and Suffolk.

Northumberland, Cumberland, Westmorland, and Durham are not described in the Survey, nor does Lancashire, as such, appear in it, though Furness and the northern part of Lancashire, as well as the south of Westmorland and a part of Cumberland are included within the survey of the West Riding of Yorkshire. The part of Lancashire between the Ribble and the Mersey, containing 688 manors, is joined to Cheshire. Part of Rutland is surveyed in the counties of Northampton and Leicester.

A third volume of *Indices* was published in 1811 by the Record Commissioners appointed in 1800, as follows:

    I. Index Locorum secundum ordinem Comitatuum.
    II. Index Locorum et Possessionum Generalis.
    III. Index Nominum Tenentium in Capite.
    IV. Index Rerum Praecipuarum.

A fourth volume of *Additamenta* followed in 1816, containing the texts of

    Exon Domesday
    Inquisitio Eliensis
    Liber Winton
    Boldon Book.

This volume included a 'General Introduction to Domesday' written by Sir Henry Ellis in 1813.

These four volumes were all large folios, and to them was added in 1833 a new and enlarged version of Ellis's *General Introduction* in two octavo volumes.

Finally in 1876 the Royal Society of Literature published the text of the Inquisitio Comitatus Cantabrigiensis and an improved text of the Inquisitio Eliensis edited by N. E. S. A. Hamilton, in quarto.

Facsimiles of the manuscripts of both volumes of Domesday Book, county by county, were issued by the Ordnance Survey in photo-zincography (1861–4).

For more adequate facsimiles see the Palaeographical Society (1873), Plates 243, 244, and the volumes of Darby's *Domesday Geography* (1954–67).

The official Breviate, that is an abbreviated text of Domesday, preserved in the Public Record Office (Miscellaneous Books [T.R], No. 284) made in the second quarter of the thirteenth century, has never been printed.

For a facsimile of a leaf of this manuscript see *Herefordshire Domesday*, ed. V. H. Galbraith and James Tait (Pipe Roll Society), 1950.

Translations of the full Domesday text, county by county, for nearly every county are provided in the *Victoria History of the Counties of England*.

OTHER WORKS

Anglo-Saxon Chronicle: ed. B. Thorpe (Rolls Series), 2 vols., 1861; ed. C. Plummer, 2 vols., 1892–9.

BALLARD, A. *The Domesday Inquest*, 1906.

—— *British Borough Charters*, vol. i, 1913; vol. ii (with James Tait), 1923.

—— *An Eleventh Century Inquisition of St. Augustine's, Canterbury*, 1920.

BARING, F. H. 'The Exeter Domesday', *E.H.R.*, 1912, p. 309.

BARLOW, F. *The Life of King Edward the Confessor* (Nelson's Medieval Texts), 1962.

—— 'Domesday Book: A Letter from Lanfranc', *E.H.R.*, 1963, p. 284.

—— *Edward the Confessor*, 1970.

BENTHAM, J. *History of the . . . Church of Ely*, 1771.

BISHOP, T. A. M., and CHAPLAIS, P. *Facsimiles of English Royal Writs to A.D. 1100*, 1957.

BLAKE, E. O. *Liber Eliensis* (R. Hist. Soc., Camden, Third Series), 1962.

BROOKE, C. N. L. *From Alfred to Henry III*, 1961.

—— *The Saxon and the Norman Kings*, 1963.

CAENEGEM, R. C. VAN. *Royal Writs in England from the Conquest to Glanville*, 1959.

CAM, HELEN M. *The Hundred and the Hundred Rolls*, 1930.

—— *Liberties and Communities in Medieval England*, 1944.

—— 'Stubbs Seventy Years After', *Camb. Hist. Journal*, vol. ix, No. 2, 1948.

CHAPLAIS, P. 'The Origin and Authenticity of the Royal Anglo-Saxon Diploma,' *Journal of the Soc. of Archivists*, Oct. 1965.

—— 'The Anglo-Saxon Chancery: From the Diploma to the Writ', ibid., Oct. 1966.

CHEW, H. M. *The English Ecclesiastical Tenants-in-Chief and Knight Service*, 1932.

CHIBNALL, A. C. *Fiefs and Fields of a Buckinghamshire Village*, 1963.

DARBY, H. C. *The Domesday Geography of England*, 5 vols., 1954–67.

—— 'Domesday Woodland,' *Econ. Hist. Review*, 1950, p. 21.

DARLINGTON, R. R. *The Vita Wulfstani of William of Malmesbury* (R. Hist. Soc.), 1928.

DAVIS, G. R. C. *Medieval Cartularies of Great Britain*, 1958.

DAVIS, H. W. C. *England Under the Norman and Angevins*, 1905.

DAVIS, R. H. C. *The Kalendar of Abbot Samson* (R. Hist. Soc., Camden Third Series), 1954.

DE RAMESEIA, R. S. *Cart. Monasterii*, ed. W. H. Hart and P. A. Lyons, 1884.

Domesday Re-bound (Public Record Office), 1954.

DOUGLAS, D. C. 'A Charter of Enfeoffment under William the Conqueror', *E.H.R.*, 1927, p. 245.

—— 'Fragments of an Anglo-Saxon Survey from Bury St. Edmunds', ibid., 1928, p. 376.

—— 'Some Early Surveys from the Abbey of Abingdon', ibid., 1929, p. 618.

—— *Feudal Documents from the Abbey of Bury St. Edmunds*, 1932.

—— *The Domesday Monachorum of Christ Church, Canterbury* (R. Hist. Soc.), 1944.

—— [with G. W. Greenaway] *English Historical Documents*, vol. ii, 1953.

—— *William the Conqueror*, 1964.

DOVE, P. E. (ed.) *Domesday Studies*, 2 vols., 1888.

EYTON, R. W. *A Key to Domesday: Analysis of the Dorset Survey*, 2 vols., 1878.

—— *Domesday Studies: Analysis of the Somerset Survey*, 2 vols., 1880.

—— *Domesday Studies: Analysis of the Staffordshire Survey*, 1881.

VON FEILITZEN, O. *The Pre-Conquest Personal Names of Domesday*, Uppsala, 1937.

FIFOOT, C. H. S. (ed.). *The Letters of Frederic William Maitland*, 1965.

FINN, R. WELLDON. 'The Evolution of Successive Versions of the Domesday Survey', *E.H.R.*, 1951, p. 561.

—— *The Domesday Inquest*, 1961.

—— *An Introduction to Domesday Book*, 1963.

—— *The Liber Exoniensis*, 1964.

—— *The Eastern Counties*, 1967.

FREEMAN, E. A. *The History of the Norman Conquest*, 6 vols., 1867–79.

GALBRAITH, V. H. 'Royal Charters to Winchester', *E.H.R.*, 1920, p. 385.

—— 'Girard, the Chancellor', ibid., 1931, p. 77.

—— 'Monastic Foundation Charters of the Eleventh and Twelfth Centuries', *Camb. Hist. Journal*, vol. iv, 205–22, 296–8.

—— 'The Making of Domesday Book', *E.H.R.*, 1942, p. 161.

—— *Studies in the Public Records*, 1948.

—— 'The Date of the Geld Rolls in Exon Domesday', *E.H.R.*, 1950, p. 1.

—— *The Making of Domesday Book*, 1961.

—— 'Notes on the Career of Samson, bishop of Worcester 1096–1112', *E.H.R.*, 1967, p. 86.

—— '1066 and All That', *Leicestershire Arch. and Hist. Soc.*, 1967.

GARMONSWAY, G. N. *The Anglo-Saxon Chronicle*, 1953.

HARMER, F. E. *Anglo-Saxon Writs*, 1952.

HEARNE, T. (ed). *Textus Roffensis*, 1720.

—— *Hemingi Chartularium*, 2 vols., 1723.

—— *Liber Niger Scaccarii*, 2 vols., 1771.

HECTOR, L. C. *The Handwriting of English Documents*, 1958.

HOYT, R. S. *The Royal Demesne, 1066–1272*, 1950.

—— 'The Terrae Occupatae of Cornwall and the Exon Domesday', *Traditio*, vol. ix, 1953.

—— 'Representation in the Administrative Practice of Anglo-Norman England', *Album Helen Cam*, vol. ii, 1961, p. 13.

—— 'A Pre-Domesday Kentish Assessment List', *Pipe Roll Soc.*, N.S. 36, 1962.

HUNT, W. 'Two Chartularies of the Priory of St. Peter at Bath', *Somerset Record Soc.*, vol. vii, No. 73, 1893, pp. 67–8.

JOHNSON, C. (ed.). *Dialogus de Scaccario* (Nelson's Medieval Texts), 1950.

KER, NEIL R. 'Heming's Cartulary', in *Studies . . . presented to F. M. Powicke*, 1948.

LENNARD, REGINALD. *Rural England (1086–1135)*, 1959.

MAITLAND, F. W. [with F. Pollock] *The History of English Law*, 2 vols., 1895 (2nd edition, 1898).

—— *Domesday Book and Beyond*, 1897.

—— *Township and Borough*, 1898.

—— [with Mary Bateson] *The Charters of the Borough of Cambridge*, 1901.

—— *The Constitutional History of England*, 1909.

—— *Collected Papers*, ed. H. A. L. Fisher, 3 vols., 1911. See also C. H. S. Fifoot (above).

MASON, J. F. A. 'The Date of the Geld Rolls', *E.H.R.*, 1954, p. 283.

LE PATOUREL, J. 'The Reports of the Trial on Penenden Heath', in *Studies . . . presented to F. M. Powicke*, 1948.

—— *The Norman Colonisation of Britain*, Spoleto, 1969.

PETIT-DUTAILLIS, C. *Studies . . . supplementary to Stubbs' Constitutional History*, vol. i, 1908.

The Pipe Roll of 31 Henry I (Pipe Roll Soc.), 1929.

POOLE, A. L. *From Domesday Book to Magna Carta, 1087–1216*, 1951.

POOLE, R. L. *The Exchequer in the Twelfth Century*, 1912.

—— *Studies in Chronology and History*, ed. A. L. Poole, 1934.

Regesta Regum Anglo-Normannorum, ed. H. W. C. Davis *et al.*, 4 vols., 1913–69.

RICHARDSON, H. G., and SAYLES, G. O. *The Governance of Medieval England*, 1963.

ROUND, J. H. *Feudal England*, 1895.

Round, J. H. *Calendar of Documents Preserved in France, 918–1206*, vol. i (1899).

Sanders, I. W. *Feudal Military Service in England*, 1956.

—— *English Baronies*, 1960.

Sawyer, P. 'The "Original Returns" and Domesday Book', *E.H.R.* 1955, p. 177.

—— 'The Place-Names of the Domesday Manuscripts', *B.J.R.L.*, vol. xxxviii, No. 2, 1956.

—— 'Evesham A', *Worcester Hist. Soc.*, 1960.

Seebohm, F. *English Village Community*, 1883.

Southern, R. W. 'The First Life of Edward the Confessor', *E.H.R.*, 1943, pp. 385–400.

—— *Place of Henry I in English History* (Brit. Acad.), 1962.

—— *Medieval Humanism and Other Studies*, 1970.

Stapleton, T. *Chronicon Petroburgense* (Camden Soc.), 1849.

Stenton, Doris M. [with Lewis C. Loyd] *Sir Christopher Hatton's Book of Seals*, 1950.

Stenton, F. M. *William the Conqueror* (Putnam's Heroes of the Nations), 1908.

—— *The First Century of English Feudalism, 1066–1166*, 1932.

—— *Anglo-Saxon England*, 1943.

Stephenson, Carl. *Borough and Town* (Med. Acad. of America), 1933.

—— *Medieval Institutions*, ed. Bryce D. Lyon, 1954.

Stevenson, W. H. 'A Contemporary Description of the Domesday Survey', *E.H.R.*, 1907, p. 74.

Stubbs, W. *Select Charters*, 1870.

—— *Constitutional History of England*, 3 vols., 1873–8.

Tait, J. Review of *Domesday Book and Beyond*, *E.H.R.*, 1897, p. 768.

—— *The Medieval English Borough*, 1936.

Taylor, C. S. 'An Analysis of the Domesday Survey of Gloucestershire,' *Bristol and Gloucester Arch. Soc.* 1888.

Tout, T. F. *Chapters in the Administrative History of Medieval England*, 6 vols., 1920–33.

—— *Collected Papers*, 3 vols., 1932–4.

VINOGRADOFF, P. *Villainage in England* (Russian, 1887), English, 1892.

—— *The Growth of the Manor*, 1905.

—— *English Society in the Eleventh Century*, 1908.

WHITELOCK, DOROTHY. *English Historical Documents*, vol. i, 1955.

WYON, A. *The Great Seals of England*, 1887.

ABBREVIATIONS

B.J.R.L.	*Bulletin of the John Rylands Library*
D.B.	Domesday Book
D.B.B.	*Domesday Book and Beyond*
E.H.R.	*English Historical Review*
F.E.	Round's *Feudal England*
H.E.L.	*History of English Law*
I.C.C.	Inquisitio Comitatus Cantabrigiensis
I.E.	Inquisitio Eliensis
M.D.B.	*The Making of Domesday Book*
M.E.B.	*Mediaeval English Borough*
S.C.	Stubbs's *Select Charters*
Trans. R. Hist. Soc.	*Transactions of the Royal Historical Society*
V.C.H.	*Victoria County History*

NOTE

In the Record Edition of Domesday Book Volumes I and II (1783) the original foliation of the manuscript has been scrupulously retained, and it was even attempted by a special record type to reproduce the original abbreviations of the manuscript. Both volumes are therefore, as it were, a facsimile in print of the original. Thus references to Volume I (which is in double column) are cited by the folio, the column, and the recto or verso of a leaf, e.g. a reference to f. 191 a 2 means that the entry will be found in the second column of the recto of the leaf so numbered in the printed edition, and a reference to f. 191 b 1 in the first column of the verso of that leaf as printed.

In the Record Edition of Exon Domesday the text is printed consecutively, though the folios are marked in the margin. References to Exon Domesday below, therefore, are to the page except in a few cases where, for special reasons, it has been necessary to quote the folio.

The two volumes of Domesday Book were published in 1783. These were followed by the volume of *Indices* in 1811; and a fourth volume of *Additamenta* in 1816, including, among other texts, the 'Exon Domesday' preserved in Exeter Cathedral, the Inquisitio Eliensis, and an elaborate 'General Introduction' compiled by Sir Henry Ellis. These four large folios, viz. two of the text, one of *Indices*, and one of *Additamenta*, were interdependent and together form what is indexed in libraries as 'Domesday Book'. A little later, in 1833, Ellis's 'General Introduction' was reissued by the Record Commission in a much-improved second edition in two octavo volumes, together with valuable indexes of 'Tenants-in-Chief and Under-Tenants'. So well and thoroughly was the work done, that only one other important publication relating

to the Survey has since been added to the original four
volumes, viz. the Inquisitio Comitatus Cantabrigiensis
and a new and better text of the Inquisitio Eliensis edited
together by N. E. S. A. Hamilton in 1876. Ellis had,
indeed, quoted largely from this twelfth-century manuscript of the I.E. in his Introduction,[1] but omitted the
text of the I.C.C. Its absence from the original publication
was later to have momentous consequences when J. H.
Round made it the cornerstone of his researches on
Domesday Book. The apparatus available today for
Domesday study was completed between 1861 and 1864,
when the Ordnance Survey issued, county by county, a
photozincographed facsimile of both volumes. Useful as
it is, this crude reproduction[2] is technically inadequate
for palaeographical scholarship; nor does it include the
vital Exon Domesday, which, it is now recognized, antedated Volume I.

It is, at first sight, somewhat surprising that the text of
Domesday Book, so ancient and so authoritative from its
completion on the death of William the Conqueror,
remained unpublished until the very end of the eighteenth
century. The explanation, or part of it, lies in the venera-
tion with which it had always been regarded, and, indeed,
still is. Within a century of its compilation it had acquired
its popular name of Domesday Book from whose verdict
there was no appeal. As late as 1381 it was constantly
cited during the Peasants' Revolt; and since then often
quoted in the House of Lords. For such legal purposes,
the king's clerks who preserved it in the Treasury, when
called upon for a transcript of any entry in it, endeavoured
to reproduce it almost in facsimile, and therefore retaining
all the abbreviations of words which characterized the
original. In 1839 the two volumes were finally lodged in

---

[1] Ellis, *General Introduction* (1833), vol. i, pp. 22 ff.
[2] In the Introduction to this facsimile, it is stated that the cost of printing
Domesday Book in 1783 had been £38,000, and 'the cost of a copy of the work
so great that few persons could afford to purchase it'.

the Public Record Office, where just such official copies are made to this day. This respect for the script of Domesday was already in the minds of the House of Lords when, in 1767, His Majesty George III, in consequence of their Address, 'was pleased to give directions for the publication, among other records, of the Domesday Survey'. At once debate arose as to how its sacred text should be printed; and after some experiments 'a facsimile type, uniform and regular, with tolerable exactness, though not with all the corresponding nicety of the original, was at last obtained, and the publication was entrusted to Mr. Abraham Farley, a gentleman of learning as well as of great experience in Records, and who had almost daily recourse to the Book for more than forty years'.[1] The work was begun in 1773 and completed in 1783, having been ten years passing through the press.[2]

Such was the invention of what has since been known as 'record type', which was as near to the original script as was humanly possible in print. The example set by Domesday Book was scrupulously followed in the publications of the Record Commission of 1800 and its successors. It still lingers on to this day, generally somewhat modified, in some of our learned publications. The more general practice now, however, is to extend all abbreviations, printing the words in full, unless there is some doubt about the termination, when the word ends with a superior mark (') above the line.

The appointment of the first Record Commission in 1800 arose from the publication of Domesday Book, and this Commission proved to be the turning-point in the publication of the national records by the State, which has ever since continued, however inadequately, to print accurate texts of the more important public records since the

[1] Ellis, *Introduction*, vol. i, p. 360.

[2] Sir William Hamilton (1730–1803), who collected pictures and rare books, was an early purchaser of Domesday Book (Winifred Gérin, *Horatio Nelson* (1970), p. 192). He also possessed the Velasquez portrait which was recently sold for more than two million pounds.

year 1199. Mr. Farley's work set a very high standard for all later state publications, and was warmly commended in these words by the Commissioners in 1800:

> The uncommon Correctness with which it is printed, proves how justly Confidence was placed in the Ability and Accuracy of the Editor. His Skill, however, in reading and explaining Records, did not induce him to depart in a single Instance from the Original, even where he found an apparent Error. He made the Copy for the Press with the same Fidelity he would have copied any Extract from the Book to be produced in a Court of Justice, preserving every Interlineation and Contraction, that he might put it out of his Hands as a faithful Transcript of the Survey.[1]

Their approval has been, I think, echoed by all who have since worked upon Mr. Farley's text; and considering the date, it was an astonishing performance.

Sir Henry Ellis was the Principal Librarian of the British Museum, and, in my judgement, his *Introduction* was a great antiquarian achievement. Looking backwards, it appears as the watershed between Domesday studies pursued for centuries before the printing of the original text in 1783, and those since, which its publication so stimulated. Ellis was the first, or one of the first, to check the conclusions of earlier writers, both medieval and modern, against the printed text, and his footnotes extensively cite their works. He also cites, in both text and footnotes, many hundreds of particular passages illustrating every aspect of Domesday touched upon in the *Introduction*. These had been brought to light during the compilation of the Indexes published in Volume III (1811), and the three additional Indexes included in the two octavo volumes published in 1833.[2] Indeed, he reminds us in the Preface to the *General Introduction* that it is in fact a new and much-improved edition of that published in Volume IV (1816). This second edition has

---

[1] *First Report on Public Records* (1800), p. 40.

[2] These have since been supplemented by O. von Feilitzen, *The Pre-Conquest Personal Names of Domesday Book* (Uppsala, 1937).

proved definitive. Since its publication (1833) hundreds of Domesday scholars have begun their studies on Ellis, and no one of equal learning since has even attempted anything comparable with it. Early cartularies, like that of Abingdon, are freely quoted; so too, the early English laws and many valuable charters from the manuscripts of the British Museum. Some of these, like the Northampton Geld Roll 1072 (Vol. I, p. 184), have deeply influenced later research; nor am I prepared to say that all these valuable documents have even today received separate publication. In this way Ellis's *Introduction* has served as almost an 'original' source for later antiquaries, who have used their Ellis to widen their acquaintance with the subject, not always with due acknowledgement. It is safe to say that today, after nearly two centuries, any serious student will profit by carefully studying Ellis's acute summaries in each particular section of his treatise.

The *General Introduction* (1833) has thus served as the gateway to research upon Domesday Book; and thereby deeply affected the conclusions of later scholars. In tone, it is entirely undogmatic, designed not to prove a thesis, but simply to illustrate in a factual way every aspect of Domesday information. That the merits of the *Introduction* have never received proper recognition is perhaps due to the way in which they are presented. There is no 'table of contents': only marginal headings, which disguise the writer's clear and logical approach to his subject. These marginal headings when set out in tabular form read as follows:

VOLUME I

II. Principal Matters Noticed in this Record

VOLUME II

With the aid of these Tables any reader can turn at once to the subject on which he wishes for information. So used, Ellis's *Introduction* is, then, still of value to historians, though, of course, it is hardly a work of 'historical research' as understood today, lacking both method and critical standards. The testimony of medieval chroniclers, in particular, is cited regardless of date. For Ellis, all chroniclers are 'free and equal', and he has a special fondness for the pseudo-Ingulph and other late chroniclers whose verdicts are entirely derivative. His last words (vol. i, p. 5) on this indefatigable compilation reflect his own feelings:

The compiler of these volumes is perfectly aware that although he has passed years of labour upon Domesday, he has only opened the way to a knowledge of its contents. Domesday Book is a mine of information which has not yet been sufficiently wrought. . . . Its metal cannot be exhausted by the perseverance of any single labourer.

I

DOMESDAY RESEARCH FROM 1833 TO THE END OF THE FIRST WORLD WAR (1918)

IN 1833, then, the Domesday canon was virtually complete, and available in print for study and comment by the amateur antiquarians, on whom historical study still largely depended. As early as 1788, for example, Robert Kelham (1717–1808) had published his *Domesday Book Illustrated*; and as the number of local history societies increased, each county acquired its separate bibliography. The publication of Domesday Book was only a part, if an important part, of a world-wide upsurge of interest in the Middle Ages, from which, within a generation, the study of history everywhere acquired academic status. Its furtherance in England passed from the hands of local amateurs to the scholars of the Public Record Office, and the British Museum, and, later still, to paid professors in the universities, who slowly learned from the expert librarians to read and handle the manuscripts. These institutions were busy sorting, arranging, and publishing catalogues of their manuscripts, inspired by the activities of the first Record Commission (1800) which gave rise to the centralization of nearly all state documents in the Public Record Office, set up in 1838 in Chancery Lane. This government-financed attack on the printing of the national records was rounded off by the inception in 1858 of the famous Rolls Series, whose prime target was the publication of the chroniclers and other narrative sources.

To trace the history of Domesday research over a period now approaching two centuries would be a difficult but rewarding task which could take a lifetime. Even here, however briefly, something must be said; for in this period the study of history has become an ever-expanding revelation, as scholars have slowly evolved a more critical and even 'scientific approach to their material. English historical scholarship has always borne the stamp of realism and a soul-saving 'common sense', but in the ancillary techniques—Paleography, Diplomatic, Textual Criticism, and so on—has never been quite abreast of our continental neighbours. Even today much of the work done on Domesday is marked by the traditional repetition of nineteenth-century dogmas no longer tenable.

The first important name in this evolution is that of the Revd. R. W. Eyton (1815–1881), author of *The Antiquities of Shropshire* and the *Itinerary of King Henry II*. He was a master of topography, and both these works are still of value to scholars. In his later years, Eyton did important pioneer work on Domesday, which has influenced all later inquiry. He was the first to realize the vital importance of the Exon Domesday, preserved in Exeter Cathedral, the text of which was obscurely tucked away in Volume IV of Domesday Book. His *Key to Domesday: Dorset* was published in 1878, and a further book dealt with Somerset. The Exon Domesday is an early draft of the Survey made by the king's *legati* or justices for the five south-western counties of Wiltshire, Dorset, Somerset, Devon, and Cornwall, which Eyton correctly identified as one of the groups of counties or circuits into which the country was divided for the carrying out of the Survey. This in itself was an advance, and led Eyton on to suggest the possible number of these circuits and the counties composing each of them. He decided that they were nine[1] in number, and though he has been much criticized, no later scholar has as yet finally settled this very important problem. But Eyton's main interest in Exon Domesday centred on the unique *Inquisitio geldi*, or

[1] *Notes on Domesday* (1880).

tax accounts of a levy of geld at 6 shillings on the 'hide', which is an integral part of the manuscript. From these sources he worked out a new theory of the *hide* as a precise fiscal unit, supporting his conclusions by elaborate statistical tables. This, his main thesis, was later, and justly, demolished by J. H. Round; and he also misdated his geld accounts.[1] But his reconstructions of the Hundreds in these counties (not identified in the manuscript), together with his researches on the 'circuits', are still the true starting-point for the understanding of the all-important, but much neglected Exon Domesday.

By the time Eyton published his *Key to Domesday*, the whole study of medieval England had been transformed by the rapid growth of the Oxford History School. The new movement can be conveniently dated from the appointment in 1866 of William Stubbs (1825–1901) as regius professor at Oxford. A staunch Anglican and a Tory, his central thesis was the Divine Government of the World, manifested by the rise of Christianity, which was for him the beginning of modern history. After thirty years of arduous preparation he wrote his famous, three-volume *Constitutional History of England* (1873–8), the greatest historical work published in England since Gibbon's *Decline and Fall of the Roman Empire*. Though Stubbs never specialized on Domesday Book, he fully grasped its importance. He taught what, I suppose, is still held today, that William the Conqueror brought 'Feudalism' into England, though his dislike of all things French led him to stigmatize it as an evil, which Henry II and his successors slowly got rid of. But though now to some extent outdated, his account of the Survey (vol. i, pp. 416–17) is firmly based on the contemporary authorities, and sticks to the facts; nor did he fail to point out the lasting influence of the Survey on later medieval history. He was, and was universally accepted as, the greatest medieval scholar of his time, though, as James Bryce

[1] See below, pp. 20–1.

pointed out, his *Constitutional History* was never easy reading owing to 'that tentative caution of phrase'[1] which characterized so much of his writing.

But if Stubbs dominated the Victorian scene, he did not do so alone. Rather he enjoyed a *condominium* with his lifelong friend Edward Augustus Freeman (1823–92), the fifth volume of whose *History of the Norman Conquest* (1867–79) included a minute and searching analysis of Domesday Book. Yet with all his learning Freeman lacked both the restraint and the wisdom of Stubbs; and his dogmatism roused resentment among the younger scholars who none the less first learned about Domesday from his book. And so the *Norman Conquest* remains to this day a great quarry of information, silently excavated by later writers more deeply influenced by his conclusions than they were aware of. Freeman succeeded Stubbs as regius professor at Oxford in 1884, when he was more than sixty years of age, and what perhaps he most lacked was the intimacy with the past arising from the study of the sources in the original manuscripts. These Freeman left severely alone, although, somewhat oddly, he was the first scholar to plead for a new edition of the Survey. 'A really critical edition of the whole Survey,' he wrote, 'bringing the full resources of modern scholarship to bear on all the points suggested by it, is an object which ought to be taken up as a national work.'[2] Who knows? Had Stubbs ever said as much, this great enterprise might well have been carried through. But Freeman's reputation died with him. Whatever the reasons—and they are complex—not the least was the venom his writings aroused in the breast of John Horace Round (1854–1928).

Beyond question, Round was the most extraordinary, as he was also the greatest, of Domesday experts. He was no professor, but, appropriately, the 'lord of a manor', who had no need to teach. He was none the less academic,

---

[1] W. H. Hutton, *William Stubbs*, p. 91.
[2] *Norman Conquest*, vol. v (1876), p. 733.

having read the History School at Balliol, and 'sat under' Stubbs, whose views he always treated with respect. Of Freeman, on the other hand, he was from the first the declared enemy; and, regrettably, his Domesday studies are permanently and inextricably interwoven with his anti-Freeman obsession. A lifelong invalid, he worked to the very end with concentrated fury, and his books are, in reality, collections of essays typical of a man whose strength lay in analysis rather than synthesis. Though Freeman was his 'King Charles's head', he dealt brutally with the errors of other scholars, and the late Professor Tout—his contemporary—once said to me that the nearest approach to a compliment he had ever had from Round was in an Index which read, 'Freeman, E. A: gross errors of', followed later by 'Tout, T. F: errors of'. In 1895, under the title of *Feudal England*, he published a large assortment of his controversial articles, of which the first 300 pages contain his Domesday studies and his famous essay on the 'Introduction of Knight Service into England'. The second half of the book deals with a score of separate historical questions to which he gave clear convincing answers. They throw a flood of light on twelfth-century feudalism, later brilliantly developed by Sir Frank Stenton in his *First Century of English Feudalism 1066–1166* (1932). *Feudal England*, it is not too much to say, revolutionized Domesday studies, and its impact was so great as to cause Professor F. W. Maitland to delay the publication of his own *Domesday Book and Beyond* until 1897. Taken together, these two volumes are the keystone of Victorian Domesday research. Both have an importance far transcending the minutiae of the Domesday statistics with which they deal. For while in Maitland's book Domesday was seen through the eyes of our greatest master of medieval law, Round's was illuminated by his genius for genealogy, a subject inseparable from the Survey, on which he wrote copiously elsewhere and which he equally revolutionized. Both authors posed the questions and defined the terms used in all later discussion; and so all later progress stems from them. 'The best of Mr. Round's merits', wrote Sir Frederick Pollock[1] in the *English Historical Review* in 1895, 'is that the next generation will never want to know how much rubbish he has swept or helped to sweep away. He has done more than any one scholar to put us in the way of reading Domesday Book aright.'

Both *Feudal England* and *Domesday Book and Beyond* had involved 'a great deal of drudgery' (as Maitland put it),[2] and represented the 'last word' of their authors on the Survey. Round's criticism of Freeman went back to 1882, and Maitland, we know, was already up to his eyes in Domesday in 1891. In fact, a great deal of *Domesday Book and Beyond* was originally intended for the *History of English Law* which Frederick Pollock and he had published in 1895. Both, too, had taken part in the great 'Domesday Commemoration' of 1886 from which came two volumes of *Domesday Studies*, dedicated (by permission) to Queen Victoria in commemoration 'of one of the greatest works of one of the greatest statesmen that ever ruled England, her Majesty's illustrious ancestor and predecessor'.[3] The second of these volumes was described by Maitland as 'a thing for the most part of naught', but to the first Round had himself contributed two outstanding articles, which still have to be read, viz. 'Danegeld and the Finance of Domesday' and 'Notes on Domesday Measures of Land'. On all sides there was much talk of 'scientific history', and the word 'Feudalism', since then so overworked, was coming into vogue. Most strange of all was the way these remote studies reflected the violent political prejudices of Victorian England. As a passionate advocate of 'democracy', not to say 'demagogy', Freeman was 'all

---

[1] The following year Pollock himself wrote 'A Brief Summary of Domesday' in the *E.H.R.*

[2] Fifoot, *Letters*, No. 107.

[3] *Domesday Studies*, ed. P. E. Dove (1888).

for King Harold', 'one whose claim was not drawn only from the winding sheet of his father', while Round's political sympathies are still preserved for us in the conclusion of his blistering article on Mr. Freeman and the Battle of Hastings! He denounced Freeman as a 'blind democrat' and a 'novus homo', for whom history 'was ever past politics'—a view Maitland seems to have shared.[1] But in imagination and historical understanding Maitland was far in advance of both of them, and in his correspondence he appears as the most detached and objective of all English medieval scholars then alive. Round's genius for sheer new discovery and Maitland's imaginative range on Domesday matters were thus entirely complementary; and following them we still look forward to the time 'far ahead, when by slow degrees the thoughts of our forefathers, their common thoughts about common things, will have become thinkable once more'.[2]

It was something of an accident that *Domesday Book and Beyond* and *Feudal England* became so closely linked together, and not altogether a fortunate one. In 1876 N. E. S. A. Hamilton published the Inquisitio Comitatus Cantabrigiensis, the only serious omission from the Record Commission publication of Domesday. Round grasped its importance as a guide to the procedure followed by the Domesday commissioners (*legati*); but he was also, perhaps, unconsciously led to exaggerate its significance because it had entirely escaped Professor Freeman's notice. The first sentence of *Feudal England* reads 'The true key to the Domesday Survey, and to the system of land assessment it records, is found in the *Inquisitio Comitatus Cantabrigiensis.*' On these ominous words, so reminiscent of Eyton's *Key to Domesday*, Round was never able to go back. They committed him to the view that the 'Original Returns' to the Survey were no more than a great series of Hundred Rolls, arranged

---

[1] Fifoot, *Letters*, No. 175.   [2] *D.B.B.*, p. 520.

geographically in the same manner as the *Rotuli Hundre-dorum* of Edward I's reign, two centuries later. This over-simplification of a most complicated process was too hastily accepted, first by Maitland and R. L. Poole and then more generally by other scholars. The only 'Key to Domesday', it scarcely needs to be said, lies in a balanced scrutiny of the whole of the contemporary evidence; and Round, having taken his stand, was faced by the insoluble problem presented by the Exon Domesday, which al-though prior to the Exchequer volume omits all reference to the Hundreds. Accordingly, in the Pedigree of Domes-day MSS. with which he concluded his Domesday studies,[1] he simply omitted Exon Domesday, with the footnote 'It will be observed that I do not touch the *Liber Exonien-sis*.' This unhappy omission misled Maitland, whose index to *Domesday Book and Beyond* contains only a single reference to Exon, and that is taken from Round.

Round lived for more than thirty years after the publi-cation of *Feudal England*, struggling against constant ill-ness, but writing with undiminished zest. Not the least important part of his output was devoted to writing Introductions, of amazing learning, for the Domesday sections of various counties for the *Victoria County History*. But his views on the composition of the Survey remained unchanged. A dozen years after *Feudal England* he still asserted[2] that the 'character, origin and object' of Exon Domesday were still an unsolved mystery. An impotent ending, surely, on a work of which he had made full use in his text. Time was to show that his sustained agnosti-cism regarding Exon Domesday was as hopeless as it was unnecessary.

Maitland's *Domesday Book and Beyond* also came in for criticism in the *English Historical Review* (1897, 768–77)

---

[1] *F.E.*, p. 146.

[2] *V.C.H. Somerset*, vol. i, p. 432; and F. M. Stenton's *William the Conqueror* (1908) perpetuated the error for thirty years in its last detailed chapter on the Compilation of Domesday Book.

at the hands of James Tait, a young scholar teaching at Manchester University. Maitland replied[1] to this review (which still requires to be read by Domesday scholars) as follows:

Dear Sir,
Will you allow me to take an unusual step and to offer you my warm thanks for the review of a book of mine which you have contributed to the *English Historical Review*? If the step is unusual (and I have never done anything of the kind before) the occasion is also unusual and in my experience unprecedented, for I have never seen a review of anything that I have written which has taught me so much or gone so straight to the points that are worth discussing. I cannot refrain from telling you of my gratitude. If ever I have to make a second edition of that book I shall have to alter many things in the light of your criticisms. Certainly this would be the case in the matter of the boroughs, and I must confess that you have somewhat shaken one [of] my few beliefs in the matter of the *manerium*, namely that this term had *some* technical meaning. I can't give up that belief all at once, but may have to do so by and by.
So repeating my thanks, I remain,
Yours very truly,
F. W. Maitland.

I never met either Round or Maitland, but James Tait later became my teacher and my master in Domesday studies until his death in 1944 at the age of eighty-two. During this half-century Tait remained the sanest, safest, and wisest authority on the Survey, and the scholars who followed him—many of them still alive—combine to reflect present-day thinking about it. There were, however, some others who were making their mark at the close of the nineteenth century. One of these was Paul Vinogradoff (1854–1925), who had come from Russia in 1883 and won Maitland's friendship. He was a scholar of prodigious learning and dominating personality; and he profoundly influenced Maitland's own work. In 1887 he published in Russia, where he was still a professor in the

[1] Fifoot, *Letters*, no. 200.

University of Moscow, a book which five years later
was translated into English under the title *Villainage in
England*. Of this book Maitland—with only the Russian
text before him—wrote prophetically: 'I have read the
footnotes, and they are enough to show me that this is a
great book destined in course of time to turn the current
of English and German learning.'[1] And he lavished such
pains on its translation into English as to make it the
most effective as well as the most fundamental of all
Vinogradoff's publications. Looking backwards it is
interesting to note how small a part Domesday Book plays
in it. For the most part it was based upon Bracton,
monastic cartularies, and the plea rolls of the thirteenth
and fourteenth centuries in the Public Record Office.
'Domesday Book' is not even mentioned in the Index,
though the work contains a careful analysis of the 'Ancient
Demesne', of which something will be said below.[2] For
both Maitland and Vinogradoff, *Villainage in England*
proved the gateway to their later Domesday studies, to
which they worked backwards from the thirteenth century,
always a dangerous thing to do. Maitland produced his
History of English Law, with Frederick Pollock in 1895,
and *Domesday Book and Beyond* in 1897;[3] Vinogradoff
his *Growth of the Manor* (1905) and *English Society in the
Eleventh Century* in 1908. Both were masters of Jurisprudence; and from this angle, their books still are essential
for Domesday students. Vinogradoff, who was an ardent
'Liberal', settled in England in 1901, where as professor
of Jurisprudence at Oxford he was the first to introduce
the continental 'seminar', in which many good scholars
were to learn their job, and of these not a few upon
Domesday research. Without Maitland's charm of style
or Round's aggressive brilliance—for Vinogradoff never
fully mastered English, either as a spoken or as a written

---

[1] Fifoot, *Letters*, No. 28.   [2] See below, pp. 123–30.
[3] Oddly omitted from the notice of Maitland in the *Concise D.N.B.* 1901–
1950.

language—his later books remain today as tombs of erudition. Indeed, they carried no very clear message; but their learning was massive; and both he and they gave a wholly new impetus towards the broader use of Domesday Book for economic and social history. But in regard to Domesday Book his influence upon Maitland, who with the modesty of genius so often yielded to his views, was not entirely beneficial.

A second name of importance is that of W. H. Stevenson (1858–1924), a scholar of more positive achievement than Vinogradoff, or, perhaps, anyone else—bar Round— of his generation. A man of genius, self-taught, and for long obscure, he became an expert philologist as well as a pioneer of English Diplomatic. When I was young, one read with attention his every article in the *English Historical Review;* and I mention him here because of the far-reaching discovery he reported in the *English Historical Review* for 1907.[1] This was an absolutely contemporary (1086) account of the Survey written by a famous scholar, Robert, bishop of Hereford (1079–95). Had this been known to Round and Maitland in 1895–7 it might have altered the course of Domesday research. But coming to light when their reconstructions were still unchallenged, it was for long little heeded or explained away. But it stands today as the earliest and most reliable record of what was done in 1086, and is wholly irreconcilable with their conclusions.

One other name (which is not found in the *Dictionary of National Biography*) is that of F. H. Baring, who in the *English Historical Review* of 1912 argued, heretically then, but correctly, that the Exon Domesday was the source of the abbreviated version in Domesday, Volume I, for the five south-western counties.

It should perhaps be stressed that this rapid review of Domesday research since the publication of Domesday Book and other related texts between 1783 and 1833

[1] *E.H.R.,* 1907, p. 74, and see *S.C.,* p. 95.

deals only with a few outstanding personalities, whose writings have deeply influenced present-day writers. Their work was supported at every stage by antiquarian research on many individual counties—like that of C. S. Taylor for Gloucestershire—and published by local societies; and to all this reference must still be made by students. For our purposes, the two names of Round and Maitland stand out as still of first importance. Of these, Round is the more difficult to use, partly because he never attempted a coherent synthesis of his many dis-coveries, both genealogical and those dealing with the details of geld assessment in Domesday Book, and partly because his writings were so widely dispersed. To this day one can never be quite sure that Round has not somewhere dealt with any difficulty with which one meets. In striking contrast, Maitland's views are still living and accessible in the *History of English Law* (all of which is his except Chapter II) and *Domesday Book and Beyond*—two great books whose authority has grown rather than diminished in the seventy years since they were published.

It remains only to mention two other scholars, whose writings are still of historical, if not strictly technical, importance to Domesday research. One of these, Frederic Seebohm (1833–1912), published his *English Village Community* in 1883, ten years before Maitland wrote. It was cold-shouldered by the dominant Germanist school of the time, but in recent years a number of young historians have revived some of his views. But all this apart, the book is a 'must' for anyone who tries to see his economic history 'whole' across the centuries; for Seebohm used his Domesday evidence in the manner of a master, relating it to both earlier and later economic history in a precocious way, having regard to the date of his book.

In the same category belongs William John Corbett (1866–1925), a Fellow of King's College, Cambridge, who never committed to writing the technical results of his lifelong researches upon Domesday. Perhaps, however, he did something better; for thanks to the persistence of the editors of the *Cambridge Medieval History*, he contributed to Volumes III and V a masterly outline of English history from the barbarian invasion to the death of King Stephen in 1154. This is still, *me judice*, the best summary for Domesday studies of what can safely be said of that dark period. In particular, the famous Chapter XV in Volume V brilliantly sketches for all of us the practical scope and contents of the Norman settlement as described in Domesday Book. It was a masterpiece of vulgarization in a uniquely difficult field, and Maitland learned a lot from Corbett.[1]

The Domesday research over more than a century, summarized above, is but a small part of the general romantic movement between 1783 and 1918, in which an England turning towards Democracy rediscovered its medieval past, hitherto dismissed as 'Gothic' and 'barbarous'. 'That the roots of the present lie deep in the past' was a liberating thought when Stubbs wrote his book. But the new awareness of continuity was then assumed to imply that the motives of modern governments were identical with those of William the Conqueror and of his Saxon predecessors. The picture painted by Victorian historians was that of a pageant, which presents contemporary outlooks in antique costume. This grievous tendency reached its height in Freeman's *Norman Conquest*, much of which is a complete anachronism.

Domesday Book, then, was no mere happy accident arising from the course of events in 1085,[2] but an inevitable result of the Norman Conquest, and the need for it increased every year as the old nobility gave way to a new

---

[1] He is mentioned in the Preface to *D.B.B.*, p. vi; cf. p. 429 n. 1 and p. 507 n. 1.

[2] As, for example, in the County of Anjou, admirably summarized in Professor R. W. Southern's *Making of the Middle Ages*, pp. 80 ff.

foreign upper class, who brought with them a more feudal relationship towards the Crown than that current in the days of Edward the Confessor. How great was the difference in the relationship may never be known, owing to the pitifully inadequate sources for Old English history; but there is ample evidence of the ever-growing confusion and bitterness which accompanied the whole-sale replacement of the English ruling class by foreigners whose baronies were tenurially so fragmented that neither they nor the Crown can have been accurately informed regarding the total wealth locked up in their widely scattered manors. Some of them held lands in many counties, and the complicated details of both their revenues and their financial obligations to the Crown were set forth in anatomical detail in the Survey, which proved to be the first fully recorded administrative achievement of the new aggressive kingship, everywhere apparent in eleventh-century Europe.[1] Seen in retrospect, it appears today as the first great step towards the bureaucratic state finally evolved in the thirteenth century. This simple but all-important fact escaped our Victorian historians. Misled by the formal procedure of hundredal juries necessary to invest it with legal authority, they saw in the Survey no more than an urge to reassess the ancient and almost annual render of the ancient geld or Danegeld. But in fact it recorded the total wealth of each of the 'king's men'—that is of the tenants-in-chief, which was invaluable to the Crown in assessing the 'incidents of feudal tenure' such as marriage, minorities, reliefs, fines, and forfeitures. The splendour of Domesday Book, Volume I, together with its careful custody ever since, is proof that it was intended for the guidance of the king's

---

[1] Though Stenton may well be right in suggesting that the precise moment selected, viz. the 'deep speech' of Christmas 1085, was the result of the failure of Cnut's threatened invasion of England in that year. A large army had been imported from Normandy and was billeted on the king's tenants-in-chief, each according to his separate wealth. Garmonsway, *The Anglo-Saxon Chronicle* (1953), p. 216, and Stenton, *Anglo-Saxon England* (1943), p. 609.

administration *in perpetuum*. And so it proved for centuries to come. All this has been slowly disentangled in the last thirty years, and opens up vistas of further discovery. The making of Domesday Book, it is now evident, was a vastly more complicated operation than was formerly realized. It is here set forth as a study in its own right, and the key to our appreciation of its dominating influence upon later medieval administrative history.

In the half-century since the close of World War I, medieval historical research has undergone a striking development. Its main centre is now found in the universities, the number of which is rapidly increasing. An elaborate system of post-graduate research, based upon the Ph.D. degree, has, grown up and with it many new periodicals. A great deal of money is now available for research students, and the sheer quantity of published work has immensely increased. Meanwhile, the whole approach to Domesday problems has widened with the rapid development of Economic, Agricultural, and what is now called 'Local' History. No single thread of continuity, such as marked nineteenth-century work, is now discernible; and far too many scholars are involved to make possible any useful summary. Here it will suffice to mention two outstanding personalities, whose published work forms a link with that of the nineteenth-century masters.

The first of these is Professor T. F. Tout, of Manchester, who in the early years of the century until his death in 1929 dominated the university scene much as Maitland and Round had done in the preceding years. Tout—like his master Bishop Stubbs—was no Domesday specialist; but, unlike Stubbs, his historical outlook was deeply influenced by the eminent French medievalists of the post-1870 generation. His importance lies in the pioneer work on English administrative history set out in his *Chapters in Medieval Administrative History*. The six volumes of this work filled a large gap in English research, hitherto devoted to constitutional or straight political history. The sovereign importance of the king's household in the development of all governmental machinery from the eleventh century onwards was bluntly set out in this work, which provided a more concrete basis for further study than the half-mythical 'mark system', however diluted. Tout's later writings administered the final *coup de grâce* to the flagrant anachronisms which had so impaired Freeman's *Norman Conquest*. There was little 'nationalism' and no 'democracy' about eleventh-century kingship, whose brutal absolutism was only qualified by the limited capacity of its household staff.

The second link-name with the generation of Round and Maitland is that of Sir Frank Stenton (1880–1967), whose *Anglo-Saxon England* (1943) revitalized the study of Old English history, and still holds the field largely unchallenged.[1] He was a pupil of J. H. Round, and his name is as closely linked with the rising University of Reading as that of Tout with Manchester. A forthright and precocious scholar, he systematically surveyed every available type of evidence about Anglo-Saxon coins, charters, wills, and laws. In these far-flung researches his own speciality was the Danelaw, with which his own family was immemorially connected. His earliest articles appeared before Maitland's death in 1906; and regrettably to the end of his life he clung to Round's incorrect reconstruction of the actual compilation of the Survey.[2] But he did more to interpret the straight history of the Norman settlement than any other scholar in his *Introductions*

[1] See the elaborate obituary notice by Doris M. Stenton in *Proceedings of the British Academy*, vol. liv, 1968 (1970).

[2] *William the Conqueror* (1908), which had been a best-seller, the last chapter of which had brilliantly summarized the views of Maitland, Round, and Vinogradoff, was universally accepted when it was published. His misplaced loyalty to his earliest sponsor, in my opinion, renders his treatment of the genesis of Domesday Book in *Anglo-Saxon England* (thirty-five years later) hesitating and indeed incorrect. It was then no longer possible to believe that the circuit returns, sent to Winchester, were in the form of Hundred Rolls.

to the Domesday sections of the *Victoria County History*,[1] which are still unrivalled and authoritative. So complete was Stenton's mastery of pre-Conquest studies that his work upon the following century—1066–1166— is today in danger of being overlooked. The vital point about *Anglo-Saxon England* is that it stopped, not at 1066, but at 1087 and was thus the first really credible explanation of the new society to which the Conquest gave birth. His *First Century of English Feudalism 1066–1166* (1932) has the same importance for its period as his Anglo-Saxon narrative in the *Oxford History of England*, published eleven years later. The result of this wide span of research has meant that much of the most significant research of the last generation upon the twelfth century is the work either of Stenton's pupils[2] or of scholars deeply influenced by his writings.

[1] Viz. Derbyshire (1905); Nottinghamshire (1906); Leicestershire (1907); Rutland (1908); Huntingdonshire (1926); and Oxfordshire (1939). He also wrote the Introduction to Lincolnshire in the *Lincoln Record Society* (1924). See the Bibliography of his writings in *Preparatory to Anglo-Saxon England*, ed. Doris M. Stenton (Oxford, 1970); also my review article on Stenton in the *American Historical Review*, vol. 76, No. 4 (Oct. 1971).

[2] e.g. Professor R. R. Darlington, whose treatment of Exon Domesday follows Stenton as closely as Stenton had followed Round. The basic error of both, as of Round, lay in their failure to explain the Exon Domesday, which was not even mentioned in Stenton's *William the Conqueror*.

II

THE SOURCES OF THE
DOMESDAY SURVEY

A. *The Contemporary Manuscripts*

DOMESDAY BOOK, or simply Domesday, arose from
the 'deep speech' which William the Conqueror
had with his 'witan' in Gloucester at Christmas
1085. The Survey (*descriptio*) was carried out in 1086,
and the final record completed, so far as it *was* completed,
by September 1087 when the king died. That all further
work upon it was halted by the Conqueror's death is only
an assumption, but a reasonable, indeed, an inevitable
one; for at that date each reign was followed by a lawless
interregnum during which the household of the late king
was replaced by that of his successor. We may guess at
what was said at Gloucester during that deep speech, but
we can never hope, at this distance of time, to know just
why this massive inquiry (*inquisitio*) was set on foot. As to
what was actually done and how it was done, on the other
hand, we are uniquely well informed by the surviving
manuscripts. The all-important fact about Domesday is
that it is our earliest public record, carefully preserved by
the officers of the king's household for more than eight
centuries, and so to be found today at the Public Record
Office, Chancery Lane, where it can be seen in the Museum. There must be some good reason to explain this
lone survivor of the Conqueror's no doubt considerable
archives. And it is not far to seek; for, in striking contrast
with later official surveys, the prudent Norman clerks at
Winchester, subordinating completeness to practical
utility, deliberately jettisoned more than half the information gathered by the king's *legati*, commissioners or

justices, compressing the mass of statistics into a single volume, albeit a large one. It was, in short, a forward-looking handy summary, made to last. And so it proved, having served ever since as a blueprint of the new society created since 1066. For this we have the authority of the 'Dialogue concerning the Exchequer' (c. 1176), which tells us that it was already popularly known as Domesday because of the finality of its testimony in all disputes, and that it was, along with the great seal, in daily use at the Exchequer.

Such, briefly, is the contemporary verdict on Domesday Book; and it is therefore something of a surprise to find, that, though regarded as a unity, it consists of two separate volumes, wholly different in scale, in script, and in provenance. For while Volume I—Great Domesday or Exchequer Domesday—was written at Winchester by a single, expert scribe, Volume II—Little Domesday[1]—was written by quite a number of non-curial and less expert scribes, whose work compares very unfavourably with the Winchester volume. Volume II is clearly a makeshift volume, instantly explained by its contents. For although getting on for half the size of Volume I, it relates only to the three counties of East Anglia (Norfolk, Suffolk, and Essex), while Volume I contains the descriptions of the thirty other English counties surveyed. Add to this that Volume II is very much more detailed than Volume I, and the conclusion is inescapable that it preserves for us the full original returns of the *legati*, of which a summarized version was intended to be added to Volume I. We must not dogmatize, but the probable reason is, surely, that the Winchester volume was halted by William I's death. This conclusion is supported by a final Latin rubric or colophon added on the last page of Volume II which, translated, reads:

In the year 1086 from the Incarnation of Our Lord, and the twentieth year of William, this Survey (*descriptio*) was made, not only of these three counties, but also of the others.

[1] See pp. 56–64 below.

William's latest and greatest administrative achievement was thus never quite completed, and Domesday Book remains to this day as actually two books, the larger written at Winchester, Volume II written on circuit by the *legati* entrusted with the Survey of East Anglia—a fact we could never have known had it survived only in later copies. The survival of both originals also supplies positive evidence of the procedure followed in the Survey, whereby, much as in the later 'general eyres', the country was divided into a number of 'circuits', each of a group of contiguous counties entrusted to a panel of royal *legati*. So much is suggested by merely looking at the vital original manuscripts; and it is confirmed by the chance but happy survival of another original manuscript made in 1086. This is the Exon Domesday, preserved in the cathedral at Exeter, and no doubt written there. It is an early draft of another circuit return, which embraced the counties of Dorset, Wiltshire, Somerset, Devon, and Cornwall, and accordingly is on a larger scale and far more detailed than the abbreviated summary preserved for us in Volume I, Great Domesday. Like Volume II or East Anglian Domesday, it is written in a variety of non-household scripts, and as in both Volumes I and II, the information is recorded throughout under the two headings of royal demesne and the lands of the tenants-in-chief. But though it contains more than 500 folios of parchment, it is clearly only a first or early draft of the local return, from which a later, finished, version, which superseded it, must have been sent to Winchester, and this explains why it was left at Exeter. Two other points should here be mentioned: first, that, large as it is, Exon is very far from complete: much has been lost; secondly, that this manuscript includes the tax returns following a special *inquisitio geldi*, of which we have no other information in the surviving manuscripts, not even those of later date. R. W. Eyton believed that this geld inquest referred to the 6-shillings-on-the-hide levy of 1084, and this error has gravely confused later work upon it. For it in fact relates to another 6-shillings levy made in 1086, whose discoveries of 'lost', i.e. unpaying, hides were used by the *legati* on this circuit. The extraordinary importance of Exon Domesday was, quite pardonably, not recognized when Domesday Book was printed in 1783; but its neglect by later scholars is less excusable. Today we owe a great deal to the late Mr. Weldon Finn[1] who spent many years in collating it with the shorter Domesday version. We also owe to him the discovery that the scribe of Volume I actually made a few entries in Exon, though we still do not know quite why or when. But at least this dates the volume as a third and invaluable original manuscript surviving from 1086.

These three official originals of the Survey—Domesday Book, Volumes I and II, and the Exon Domesday—are the primary sources of all Domesday interpretation. There are besides certain other Domesday manuscripts of private provenance and later date which provide valuable evidence regarding the circuit proceedings. Of these the most important are the so-called Inquisitio Comitatus Cantabrigiensis and the Inquisitio Eliensis. Both manuscripts are dated by their script as midtwelfth century, and throw light on the proceedings of the East Anglian circuit and that which included Cambridgeshire and Hertford. They probably descend from discarded, preparatory drafts, left behind like Exon Domesday by the *legati* or otherwise acquired by interested parties. This is a recurrent medieval phenomenon, and long afterwards we find the Abbey of St. Albans working from an incomplete draft of Magna Carta (1215). The king's records, we are apt to forget, had not yet become the '*public* records', and contemporaries were hard put to it to discover what was happening. But the I.C.C. and the I.E. are somewhat dubious sources, since they preserve only an interim record of the circuit proceedings, not yet 'finalized'.

The tally of Domesday sources is rounded off first by the literary evidence of contemporaries, which must be carefully distinguished from the garbled accounts in later chronicles; and secondly by a large number of local, monastic compilations, now usually called 'Domesday Satellites'. Most of these are in print, and they provide a great field for future inquiry. But they are attended by the same difficulties of interpretation as the I.E. and the I.C.C. and to a much greater degree.

Such, then, are the original manuscript materials for Domesday research, all of which pose delicate and not altogether solvable problems.

B. *The Contemporary Literary Sources*

The good fortune which has left us with three original manuscripts of the Survey of 1086 is balanced by an equally and absolutely contemporary literary account[1] written by a great scholar in that very year. To anyone familiar with medieval chronicles this is even more unusual than the survival of the original texts. For much of what we class as 'contemporary' literary evidence is anonymous, and often some or even many years later than the events it narrates. This unimpeachable evidence is found in a little Latin book on Chronology, written by Robert, bishop of Hereford (1079–95), who was the close friend of the saintly Wulfstan, bishop of Worcester, the editor of the chronicle 'Marianus Scotus', and an important tenant-in-chief of William I, to whom he owed the military service of fifteen mailed knights. Moreover, we still have the original charter of 1085, by which he subinfeudated to Roger de Lacy the village of Holme Lacy, as his father had held it, that is, by the service of two knights, part of the bishop's larger quota.[2] It would be difficult to imagine a man better fitted to

---

[1] Published by W. H. Stevenson, *E.H.R.*, 1907, p. 74.
[2] *E.H.R.*, 1929, pp. 353 ff.

testify on the Survey. In the course of his book he remarks, almost incidentally, that he is writing in the year 1086,[1] when in

the twentieth year of his reign, by order of William, King of the English, there was made a survey (*descriptio*) of the whole of England, that is to say, of the lands of the several provinces of England, and of the possessions of each and of all the magnates. This was done in respect of plough land and habitations, and of men both bond and free, both those who dwelt in cottages and those who had houses and some arable land and in respect of ploughs and horses and other animals; and in respect of the services and payments due from all men in the whole land. Other investigators (*inquisitores*) followed the first; and men were sent into provinces which they did not know, and where they were themselves unknown, in order that they might be given the opportunity of checking the first survey, and, if necessary, of denouncing its authors as guilty to the king. And the land was vexed with many calamities arising from the collection of the royal money.

As evidence, Bishop Robert's concise, forthright description of the events of 1086 is on the same level as the three surviving original Domesday texts, and our reconstruction of the Survey must somehow harmonize the evidence of these four prime sources. There were, he says, two separate Inquests in 1086, of which the first was a geld inquest and the second the Domesday survey; and together they caused an immense outcry from the collection of the royal taxes. His statements are wholly at variance with the teaching of both Round and Maitland for whom the Domesday survey was a purely fact-finding royal commission intended to pave the way for a future reassessment of the geld, which had last been exacted in 1084 at the rate of 6 shillings on the 'hide'. This explanation, though inadequate even when first advanced, is wholly untenable in the light of Bishop Robert's evidence, which only came to light in 1907, when Maitland was dead and Round had long since said his 'last word' on

[1] *E.H.R.*, 1907, p. 74.

Domesday Book. True, Round stuck to his reconstruction after W. H. Stevenson's discovery. But the whole Victorian thesis fell, as it was bound to fall, like a house of cards in the next generation, when the evidence of Exon Domesday was found to corroborate the Bishop's words. There was another 6-shilling geld in 1086, preceded by an *inquisitio geldi*, and the Domesday commissioners did use its findings to exact payment from long 'lost hides' which had hitherto escaped taxation.[1] It is safe to say that had Stevenson's discovery occurred half a century earlier the whole history of Domesday research would have been very different. As early as 1888, Round had come near to the truth when he asserted that the geld was collected much more often in the period 1066–1100 than Stubbs had thought. He was quite right, but might safely have gone further still, for by the close of William I's reign the geld had once more become an annual or almost annual levy, as the first folio of Staffordshire Domesday clearly implies. The king, it says, has his geld from all the in- habitants of Stafford every year—'Rex habet de omnibus geldum per annum' (f. 246, col. 1).

The only other contemporary literary evidence about the Survey is the classic passage in the Anglo-Saxon Chronicle. I say contemporary because, though anony- mous, the writer, recording the death of William I, writes:

> If anyone desires to know what kind of man he was or how many lands he was lord over, then shall we write of him as we have known him, who have ourselves seen him and at one time dwelt in his court.

In Professor Garmonsway's modernization[2] it reads:

> The King spent Christmas (1085) with his councillors (*witan*) at Gloucester and held his court there for five days, which was followed by a three-day synod held by the archbishop and the clergy . . .

---

[1] V. H. Galbraith, 'The Date of the Geld Rolls in Exon Domesday', *E.H.R.*, 1950, p. 1.   [2] Garmonsway, p. 216.

After this the King had important deliberations and exhaustive discussions (deep speech) with his council (*witan*) about this land and how it was peopled and with what sort of men. Then he sent his men all over England into every shire to ascertain how many hundreds of 'hides' of land there were in each shire, and how much land and live-stock the King himself owned in the country, and what annual dues were lawfully his from each shire. He also had it recorded how much land his archbishops had, and his diocesan bishops, his abbots and his earls, and—though I may be going into too great detail—and what or how much each man who was a land holder here in England had in land or in live-stock, and how much money it was worth. So very thoroughly did he have the inquiry carried out that there was not a single 'hide', not one virgate of land, not even—it is shameful to record it, but it did not seem shameful for him to do—not even one ox, not one cow, nor one pig which escaped notice in his survey. And all the surveys (writings) were subsequently brought to him.

The next entry in the Chronicle covers the events of 1086,[1] including the oath at Salisbury on 1 August, and continues:

From thence he journeyed to the Isle of Wight, because he purposed to go to Normandy, and so he did thereafter. *First, however, he did as he was wont, he levied very heavy taxes on his subjects, upon any pretext, whether justly or unjustly.* He journeyed thereafter into Normandy, etc.

In this itinerary, the words printed in italics echo and confirm the more precise testimony of Robert of Hereford, which it clothes, as only the English chronicle can, with personal feeling. The chronicler's impression of the Survey in one of mingled admiration and resentment: admiration for a king strong enough to carry it out; resentment still felt by the clergy compelled to disclose their total assets. The bishops and abbots, we know, had suffered severely from William I's new imposts regarding knight service, and also from his growing avarice in his

---

[1] Ibid., pp. 216, 217.

later years. On this the chronicler comments bitterly a little later in his obituary of the king:

> The King, and the leading men were fond, yea, too fond, of avarice: they coveted gold and silver, and did not care how sinfully it was obtained, so long as it came to them. The King granted his land on the hardest terms and at the highest possible price. If another buyer came and offered more than the first had given, the King would let it go to the man who offered him more. If a third came and offered still more, the King would make it over to the man who offered him [most of all]. He did not care at all how very wrongfully the reeves got possession of it from wretched men, nor how many illegal acts they did; but the louder the talk of law and justice, the greater the injustices committed. Unjust tolls were levied and many other unlawful acts were committed which are distressing to relate.[1]

All this and much more was brushed under the carpet by the Victorian historians who at the celebration of the 800th anniversary of Domesday Book in 1886 pictured William as the beneficent prototype of Queen Victoria.[2] So he was, as the Anglo-Saxon chronicler admits; for, by and large, he was good to the Church and kept good order in the land, he says. But his 'statemanship' had nothing in common with that of the Victorians, being directed in a barbarous age towards the enrichment of the Crown and the strengthening of its control over the magnates on whose support he depended. These were the direct, twin motives of the Domesday Survey; for he lived in a world totally different from ours, and one not even yet fully comprehensible.

Why, one is tempted to ask, did the Anglo-Saxon chronicler fail to mention explicitly the geld inquest of 1086? To this the answer is twofold. First, that in those days governments were not called upon to explain their actions, and when they did so, it was generally done as propaganda. Secondly, that the financial extortion of

---

[1] Garmonsway, p. 218.   [2] Above, p. 6.

William's reign, if we may judge from the chronicler's words, rose in his last years to a frightful climax, ended only by his death. It was the peasantry only who suffered severely from 6-shilling gelds, since the demesnes of the tenants-in-chief were exempted. The Anglo-Saxon chronicler airs the views of the higher clergy—bishops and abbots who were tenants-in-chief. To him the Survey seemed to be an outrage, while the geld in the same year was taken for granted.

c. *The Administrative Background*

England in 1066 was an ancient monarchy, rich, vigorous, and already a 'national' state in the making. Administratively, it was a collection of shires, very much the same as it is shown today in a school atlas. Starting with Alfred the Great, these had been organized and harnessed to the central authority by a succession of able warrior kings in the tenth century. The second wave of Danish invasions and King Canute's conquest, it is now recognized, so far from having undone this achievement, endorsed and, on balance, strengthened it, so that today this time of troubles is seen as no more than an interlude arising from the personal failure of King Aethelred and the consequent disputes as to the royal succession. This is a matter of importance, since a generation ago, under the influence of J. H. Round's work, it was widely thought that the eleventh century in England was a period of decadence moving towards final and inevitable conquest. The Norman Conquest proved, in fact, final; but it was not inevitable, and the prize when won quickly became the most effective military power in Western Europe. The reign of William I coincided with a period of revolutionary change in Europe, in which the Papacy under Gregory VII vastly exalted the authority of the Church. William I, whose invasion of England had had the papal blessing, was of course deeply involved in all this, but the Norman Conquest and the rise of the Papacy were linked only by coincidence in time.

It is even arguable that England in 1066 was the most efficiently organized state in Europe. It was very much larger than Normandy, which was about the size of East Anglia; and though much smaller than France, it was more closely knit, and both the power and the wealth of its monarchy greater than that of France. It is with this administrative structure that the Domesday student is particularly concerned, the fine quality of which is, in fact, largely known to us from Domesday itself. On almost every page evidence is found of the vitality of the shire, with its shire court and its royal sheriff to direct the justice done there. Still more remarkable, and no less vigorous, is the court of the smaller divisions of each shire into Hundreds or (in Danish districts) Wapentakes. Some of these, but no more than a small minority, were before 1066 in 'private' hands, such as the eight and a half Hundreds of the liberty of the abbot of St. Edmund's Abbey. These, too, had their courts of justice, and their royal bailiffs; and already both shires and Hundreds were quasi-communities, with their suitors and, as it were, their collective personality. This intensity of local life was closely connected with that unique prerogative of Anglo-Saxon England, viz. the precocious development over centuries of the vernacular not only as a literary language but as the language of secular business and of the Church. It arose, no doubt, from the shortage of Latin-literate 'clerks', and was abandoned after 1066 when Latin took its place for business, and French as the spoken language of polite society. This in turn degraded English for three centuries to the status of a peasant patois, which soon meant the language of villeinage and the unfree—perhaps the most important of all the long-term results of the Conquest. And with this change went, as we now can see, the slow decline of both the shire and hundred courts in favour of the central justice of the king's court, which within a century and a half became the Common Law of England. But in 1086 all this still lay in the future, and the Domesday Survey was put together and hammered out in sessions of each county court, reinforced by the testimony of the relevant Hundreds and representatives of each village in the Hundred. Now, what the Survey reveals, for we should hardly have known it otherwise, is that this testimony of the Hundred was everywhere given by a sworn jury, which spoke for the whole Hundred. The historians of law assure us that this sworn inquest was first introduced into England in 1066, but their chief argument is no more than the argument from silence, which is a poor one as the change-over to Latin must have led to the neglect and eventual destruction of great quantities of Anglo-Saxon archives. That the Normans, whose prime object was to ascertain just who held what land and how *before* 1066, should have thought up and then imposed on men of middle rank in society, some of them English, a new and strange machinery of the Hundred is, surely, unlikely. And one is tempted to wonder whether both the 'reeve, the priest and six men from each village' and the sworn jury of each Hundred do not both go well back into the Anglo-Saxon past. However that may be, Domesday Book richly illustrates the often heated debates which attended the proceedings of the Survey as much of which must have been in English as in French.

Beneath the shire and the Hundred was the village, the basic unit of early agriculture, and, the towns apart, the source of all wealth. The normal village had its lord and its halimote, and the village community cultivated the land according to the open field system, the ploughed land being divided between the lord's demesne and the tenants' strips. In the time of Edward the Confessor, these ceorls or churls were, nominally, free men with wergilds of 200s., for Domesday records many slaves (*servi*). Nor were they a homogeneous body, for they are separately recorded in three main categories of villeins, bordars, and cottars. But while the village community answered for village arrangements through its reeve, priest, and six men, more often than not the village was divided into two or more separate estates, called in Domesday 'manors' or *mansiones*.

Such was the local structure of society, which was linked to the king's household, itself itinerant, from the early eleventh century by what was later called a 'chancery' department where the 'king's priests' issued to the shire courts vernacular writs sealed with a two-faced wax pendent seal. Royal interests were represented in these nerve-centres of local life by the king's sheriffs who transmitted to the royal Treasury at Winchester the fines of justice, the fixed county 'firm', and the many other annual tenders or customs due to the Crown of which the chief was the geld, whose origin lay in the first Danish invasions. It was assessed at so much—2s., 4s., 6s., for it varied—on every hide, which was traditionally the acreage needed to support a family. An eighth-century document, the so-called Tribal Hidage, sets out the total assessment of whole tribes and peoples, but by the eleventh century every village had its separate assessment. The normal Domesday entry begins with the name of the village and the number of hides for which its owner answered, and the whole system was already so ancient that this fixed village assessment was in fact often quite arbitrary. This village hidage assessment was the basis not only of geld collection but of the whole pre-Conquest military organization—the fyrd. The 'hide' in short dominated Old English local arrangements, and Domesday Book affords endless material for its further study. But more important for the Domesday student is the introduction of knight service into England from the moment William conquered the country. Mercenaries apart, the backbone of his armies were the mailed, mounted knights; and to enable his Norman vassals to provide an army in England, he gave them the lands lost by English thegns, who were almost entirely superseded by foreign barons, the greatest of whom were created 'earls'. The total lands of each baron wherever situated were treated as a single whole, his barony, in return for which he provided a quota of knights. There thus came into existence a great nexus of Honorial Courts in which William's vassals judged their own sub-tenants, among whom the tenant-in-chief distributed part at least of his quota of knights owed to the Crown. But these new franchise courts did not exempt the new baronage from their suit to the county courts, which remained the active centre of local justice and administration.

The local administrative background sketched above explains what Ellis in his *Introduction* (1833) called 'the mode of execution' followed by the Domesday Commissioners. It was as a matter of course carried out in the county court, where the lands of land-holders were gone over Hundred by Hundred, village by village, so that when completed every hide, indeed every acre of land in England, had been accounted for. That this was the procedure followed by the *legati* on each circuit is not in doubt. But the method employed to arrive at the facts must not be confused with the resulting local return, whose objective is clearly set out on the first page of each county in both Great Domesday (Vol. I) and Little Domesday (Volume II), which was in origin just one of these local returns. The purpose of the Survey was simply this—a detailed return of the rents and resources of first, the king's own demesne lands, followed by that of his archbishops, bishops, earls, barons, and other tenants-in-chief—whose names are set out in a numbered list at the head of each county. From it both the sheriffs of the separate counties and the king's chamberlains at Winchester could see at a glance the wealth of the royal demesne and that of his tenants-in-chief in each county. For while England retained both for justice and taxation its immemorial administration by counties and Hundreds, we have no written record before Domesday Book of the wealth of the king's fighting tail of feudal 'barons'.[1] Accordingly the *legati* collected the facts by the ancient machinery of shire, Hundred, and village—but made out their return to Winchester in what we now call a feudal form. In so doing they brought into English law the new legal doctrine that every acre of English land was either held by the king himself as demesne, or held directly from him by named tenants-in-chief.

Thus the united evidence of the three original manuscripts, of the contemporary literary sources, and of the administrative structure of England suggests simply that the object of the Domesday Survey of 1086 was Volume I of Domesday Book, which was an official abbreviation of returns made in precisely the same form by the local circuits, which included much additional detail, deliberately sacrificed at Winchester in the interests of practical utility. Before we examine the Survey in more detail it remains only to add that the process of its composition was misunderstood for nearly a century by Eyton's misleading analysis of the geld accounts in Exon Domesday, which seems to have been the immediate source of the strange Victorian obsession—that the sole purpose of the Survey was the 'search for geld'. Alternatively, had Stevenson's discovery of Bishop Robert of Hereford's precise evidence come to light a hundred years earlier, E. A. Freeman might well have put future research on the right lines in his *Norman Conquest*.

[1] Nearly a century later, in 1166, some of the tenants-in-chief stated that their ancestors had been enfeoffed by William I *sine carta*, i.e. not by a written charter.

III

THE MODE OF EXECUTION

A. *The Terms of Reference*

IN the customary and aristocratic society of the eleventh century, kings were under no obligation to explain their intentions to any wider circle than that of their direct vassals. The Domesday Survey was undertaken as a result of the 'deep speech' that William I had with his 'witan' at Christmas 1085, and the *legati*, barons, or commissioners who executed it acted under his personal orders and were responsible to him alone. To think of them as 'civil servants' is an anachronism, since the lesser functionaries who actually did the work were the servants of the king's domestic household, identical in kind with those of the great tenants-in-chief on whom he depended. The Pope, it is true, with false modesty officially described himself as 'a slave of the slaves of God' (*servus servorum Dei*) and the king as king only 'by the grace of God' (*dei gratia*), but, subject to these verbal reservations, both acted, or tried to act, as invested with sovereign authority. The recorded Survey, Domesday Book, was therefore not yet a 'public record', but a record of the king's household: and it is therefore no matter for surprise that our three original manuscripts—the two volumes of Domesday and the Exon Domesday—make no mention of the authority for, or the occasion of, their compilation. Rather, they plunge straight *in medias res*; and we are left to disentangle the procedure used by the *legati* simply from the final document which emerged. Yet the *legati* must have had some written terms of reference to justify their actions to all concerned, and by almost incredible good fortune this document was preserved and remains the vital key to the whole operation. It was, of course, in Latin, and translated runs as follows:

Here follows the inquest of lands (*inquisitio terrarum*), as the King's barons made it, to wit: by the oath of the sheriff of the shire and of all the barons and their Frenchmen and of the whole Hundred, of the priest, the reeve (*prepositi*), six villagers (*villani*) of each village. In order, what is the manor (*mansio*) called? Who held it in the time of King Edward? Who now holds it? How many hides? How many ploughs on the demesne? How many men? How many villagers? How many cottars? How many slaves (*servi*)? How many free men? How many socmen? How much wood? How much meadow? How much pasture? How many mills? How many fish ponds (*piscinae*)? How much has been added or taken away? How much, taken together, it was worth and how much now. How much each free man or socman had or has. All this at three dates, to wit, in the time of King Edward and when King William gave it and as it is now. And if it is possible for more to be had than is had.[1]

Here then, we have Domesday Book in a nutshell, and *before* it was made. From it we may even anticipate the form as well as the content of the Survey. The *legati* thought in terms of the county, which was the unit of their inquiry, and the county court was the scene of their proceedings. The procedure was to be that of the 'sworn inquest' conducted in a reinforced county court at which each Hundred would corporately supply the detailed statistics of ownership of all its constituent villages, and the priest and the reeve and six men from each village would be there to check its accuracy. In theory at any rate, the proceedings would be oral, the spoken word, and each 'baron' and each of his Frenchmen (which seems to refer to their sub-tenants) would agree to the statement made of his holding. Within the Hundred, the basic unit was the village, but as the ownership of many villages was divided between several manorial lords, the *legati* were instructed to list separately all manors (*maneria*, also called *mansiones*) which seem to have meant separately farmed estates. But these terms are French in origin and since we know little about them before 1086 we should

[1] I.C.C., ed. Hamilton, p. 97.

not be too meticulous in attempting to define them. On the strength of these terms of reference we can dismiss the view, once held, that the *legati* toured the shire to gather the verdicts of each Hundred. Finally, with the hindsight afforded us by Domesday Book itself, we can define exactly the meaning of the all-important question 'Who holds the manor?'. For the *legati*, the holders of land (*tenentes terras*) were the tenants-in-chief, the king's immediate vassals. They assumed—and this assumption is first known to us from Domesday Book—that all manors, indeed every acre of land in England, was 'held' either by the king or by a tenant-in-chief. The terms of reference in short look forward to Domesday Book in exactly the form in which it is cast. The Normans were never so feudal as when they arrived in England, and they silently imposed upon an England, which like Topsy had 'just growed' over the centuries, the more developed, purely contractual conception of the fee (*feodum*), the 'barony' or the honour, held directly of the Crown in return for a quota of knight service and the tangled customary renders to the king as they had obtained in Normandy— reliefs, wardships, marriages, and voluntary aids (*auxilia*).

Such was to be, and was, Domesday Book, which, as a register of tenants-in-chief, has nothing as such to do with geography, or for that matter with military service, or with the assessment or collection of geld. All these things were well known to the king. The sole purpose of the Survey was Domesday Book, a fact-finding sworn inquisition intended to portray the new feudal set-up of England as seen from the king's point of view and that of his supporting magnates: a summary, in short, of the wealth of all England and the details of its ownership. Such a far-seeing act of statemanship required, according to medieval ideas of legality, the endorsement of all who would be affected by it in the future. Hence, I think, the elaborateness of the procedure, and the extensive use of the sworn jury, which, as we have seen, the historians of law assure us was first brought to England by William the Conqueror.[1] However that may be, later English kings so extended its application in legal procedure that it became the corner-stone of English 'justice', while falling into disuse abroad. Historians of this period should not take it too seriously, for it was not till the Middle Ages were past that the freedom of the individual was closely linked with the notion of the jury. More than half of Law in these times *was* procedure, and much of it disguised the despotic measures taken to buttress royal administration. Thus, the Inquisitions *post mortem*[2] and the *proofs of age*, two vast *fonds* of royal government preserved in the Public Record Office, were of this bogus character and little more than 'common form'. These both involved the use of a jury who, in theory, testified to the complicated details of a deceased magnate's property, which, in fact, could only be known to his steward and the local escheator. It was perhaps the only way then that justice could be *seen* to be done. Such, I think, was its purpose in 1086, when most of the information was supplied by skilled clerks, and other experts, both literate and illiterate. The terms of reference speak simply of the 'oath of the *whole* Hundred', implying that the Hundred had already a 'corporate' personality, and so collectively could give assent to all that was done, however it *was* done.

It is a striking fact that no mention is made in the terms of reference to the towns, which again emphasizes the feudal, contractual character of the Survey. The Survey assumed the towns to be either royal demesne or the property of some tenant-in-chief. The *legati*, it would seem, were often puzzled by this omission, and it was only in Domesday itself (Vol. I) that the county towns were described on the first folio of the county, before or beside the list of named tenants-in-chief. Some of our

---

[1] Above, p. 29.

[2] C. G. Crump, 'A Note on the Criticism of Records', *B.J.R.L.* vol. viii (1924), pp. 140–9.

oldest towns by these brief notes enter recorded history.
But the two greatest—London and Winchester—were
silently omitted; no doubt because they presented too
large a task to be discharged in the short time available.
It should also be noted that no return of stock—cattle,
sheep, and pigs—is called for, though as the Anglo-
Saxon chronicler remarks, it was generally and very
properly recorded by the *legati* as an important component
of manorial rent or value. In Volume I of Domesday
Book, the record of such stock was everywhere omitted;
a small but significant indication that the Domesday
Survey was intended from the very outset to serve as a
permanent guide for future use by the king's household.
The terms of reference, in fact, tally exactly with the
facts recorded in the final Domesday, where they are set
out county by county, in the same way as they had been
assembled by the *legati*. They thus served as the warrant
for the proceedings of the *legati* in each county court,
which was the uniform unit of the Survey. We know,
however, from the survival of Volume II of Domesday,
and from Exon Domesday, that the *legati* were allotted
not one but a group of neighbouring counties, in each of
which the procedure laid down in the terms of reference
was repeated, and that each panel returned to Winchester
the findings of their total assignment. If we may judge by
Volume II of Domesday and from Exon these returns
each formed a single volume. But the possibility remains
that in some cases the *legati* returned their record of each
county as it was completed. However they made their
return, each *panel* had its own particular 'circuit', and
scholars have laboured at the task of defining these
circuits. To them we must next turn.

B. *The Circuits*

R. W. Eyton a century ago attempted to list the
county circuits; and his work was later used by Adolphus

Ballard. More recently they have been reviewed by Carl Stephenson, an American scholar, whose reconstruction is as follows:[1]

I. Kent (1), Sussex (2), Surrey (3), Hampshire (4), Berkshire (5)

II. Wiltshire (6), Dorsetshire (7), Somersetshire (8), Devonshire (9), Cornwall (10)

III. Middlesex (11), Hertford (12), Buckingham (13) Cambridge (18), Bedford (20)

IV. Oxford (14), Northampton (21), Leicester (22), Warwick (23)

V. Gloucester (15), Worcester (16), Hereford (17), Stafford (24), Shropshire (25), Cheshire (26)

VI. Huntingdon (19), Derby (27), Nottingham (25), Rutland (29), York (30), Lincoln (31)

VII. Essex (32), Norfolk (33), Suffolk (34)

The numbers following the name of the county refer to the order of its appearance in Volume I of Domesday Book, while No. VII, though in origin a circuit return, was never incorporated in Volume I and is now Volume II of Domesday Book. Only two others out of Stephenson's seven circuits are certainly correct, viz. I and II. The rest are no more than intelligent guesswork, on which opinion can legitimately vary, e.g. regarding Staffordshire, which some would put in circuit No. IV. My own doubts centre on No. VI, which was an immense assignment for a single circuit. It could be that Yorkshire and Lincoln formed a circuit on their own. The shires were old, historic divisions, each with its own history; and in our efforts to distinguish the circuits we are at all times balancing two factors: one, the tendency of the *legati* to impose a certain uniformity of procedure, nomenclature, and formulas; the other, the age-long difference in custom between even neighbouring counties. We have also to

[1] C. Stephenson, *Medieval Institutions*, ed. Bruce D. Lyon (1954), pp. 184–205.

bear in mind that the compilers of Volume I of Domesday Book seem to have ironed out many local variations of phrase. The most recent and detailed study of local differences is to be found in the five regional volumes of Professor H. C. Darby's *Domesday Geography of England*. We know neither the number nor the names of the *legati* or justices who formed most of these circuits, and in one instance only do we know the names of the full panel. This was No. V whose members were Remigius, bishop of Lincoln, earl Walter Giffard, Henry de Ferrers, and Adam, brother of Eudo, the king's *dapifer*.[1]

c. *The Making of the Circuit Returns*

The terms of reference, so fortunately preserved for us, were never part of the royal archives. They are a purely accidental survival, found in a twelfth-century manuscript of private provenance. This is the so-called Inquisitio Eliensis printed by Ellis in the *Additamenta* volume (No. III) of Domesday in 1816. It is not in fact an inquisition or survey, but a sort of private Domesday compiled by the Abbey of Ely from the full returns of three different circuits. Exactly when it was compiled is not known, but it seems probably to have been made either in 1086–7 or 1093,[2] not from copies of the final returns to Winchester but from early drafts of the circuit returns the *legati* left behind them, much as Exon Domesday passed into private hands, when the final return to Winchester was completed. The Abbey of Ely's lands were situated in counties divided between three different circuits, viz. Hertfordshire and Cambridgeshire in circuit No. III, Huntingdonshire in circuit No. VI, and in Essex, Norfolk, and Suffolk, circuit No. VII. That the I.E. was based on the circuit returns for manors in Cambridgeshire and Huntingdonshire is proved by the fact that they contain

---

[1] *Heming's Cartulary*, ed. Thomas Hearne (1723), vol. i, p. 288.
[2] *M.D.B.*, pp. 141–2.

detailed information omitted from Volume I of Domesday
Book. The Ely manors in East Anglia appear in much
the same form as in Volume II, which was itself in origin
the return of circuit No. VII, but the inclusion of Burgh
Apton, an Ely manor in Norfolk, shows that the source
was an earlier draft than Volume II itself, which omits to
mention it. In the same manuscript (Cotton MS. Tiberius
A VI) is another text of great importance, called the
Inquisitio Comitatus Cantabrigiensis, which Ellis, though
he saw it, failed to print. This omission was remedied in
1876 by N. E. S. A. Hamilton, who published both
texts, with scholarly care, and collated them with the
final texts found in Domesday Book, Volumes I and II.
Hamilton's book escaped Professor Freeman's knowledge,
but was exhaustively analysed by J. H. Round who based
his whole conception of the 'original returns' to Winchester upon it.[1] His work is still of the greatest value, for it
contains the record of many of his Domesday discoveries
—but his main conclusion, viz. that the original circuit
returns to Winchester were a great series of Hundred
Rolls, arranged geographically, was too hasty, and disguised their true character for half a century.

   Without going into detail, the problem must here be
summarized,[2] and the true relation of the I.C.C. to the
Survey of 1086 clarified. The I.C.C. is a single, unique
survival of the procedure followed in the Cambridge
circuit (III). It deals with the Hundreds of Cambridgeshire consecutively, beginning with a list of the eight
jurymen of Staploe Hundred who swore (*juraverunt*), and
ending imperfectly with that of North Stow. After the
names of the jury (beginning with Staploe) are set out
successively, manor by manor, the particulars of the
ownership, number of hides, ploughs, meadow, pasture,
etc., a little fuller than we have them in Volume I of
Domesday; and Round proved to demonstration that in
this circuit the 'verdict' of the Hundreds were actually

---

[1] *F.E.*, pp. 1–16.   [2] See *M.D.B.*, Chapter IX.

committed to writing by the *legati*. The I.C.C. is thus of extraordinary interest as the only surviving evidence of exactly what the terms of reference implied by the 'oath of the whole Hundred', and brings home to us as nothing else can the complexity of the task the *legati* had to deal with. There were fourteen Hundreds in Cambridgeshire, from each of which a jury of eight men, half French and half English, had to give their evidence in the county court. I have not counted how many villages there were in Cambridgeshire, but in Staploe Hundred, the first mentioned, there were about a score and, as many of these were divided between several holders, a far larger number of 'manors'—all separately assessed in 'hides'. So, as there were fourteen Hundreds, we shall be safe in saying that 'the reeve, the priest, and six villagers' from every village must have required the attendance in the county court of some hundreds of village representatives, who again are repeatedly referred to in Great Domesday as testifying to the facts in court. Clearly, having regard to the difficulties of travel and lodging in those days, the circuit officials must have had a back-breaking job, summoning and examining so many people from such different walks in life. We can only guess that the court sat for weeks on end dealing with the separate Hundreds one by one, the necessary 'personnel' having been summoned some time in advance to appear on a day set. All this must have been a very tall order indeed, and many counties were far larger than Cambridgeshire, and perhaps more difficult to deal with. East Anglia, in particular, was obviously a tremendous assignment, because of its many small free men and socmen, and its unique 'leet' organization for collecting the geld. No wonder then, if, as we are forced to believe, its local return, now Domesday Book, Volume II, arrived too late for abbreviation and inclusion in Volume I. Some, as noted above,[1] have thought that the *legati* toured their

[1] p. 35.

counties and took the local testimony in successive hundred courts. But the terms of reference call for the whole elaborate process to be carried out in the shire court of each county, and all the other evidence points to the same conclusion.

A second and even more daunting difficulty is raised by the very minuteness and thoroughness of the information gathered by the *legati*. In the oral and customary society of the eleventh century, historians love to insist on the unfogged memories of these unsophisticated yokels or warriors. But no one who has ever studied the maze of statistics preserved in Volume I of Domesday—not to speak of the fuller statistics of Volume II and of Exon Domesday—can be expected to believe that all this oral testimony, given on oath, can have been carried in the heads of those who gave it. No magnate is likely to have known just how many manors he owned in any county, let alone in a whole circuit; nor can the humbler men have recited from memory the statistics of villeins, borders, cottars, ploughs, hides, and slaves, etc. We are driven to conclude that behind the oral procedure in court, which is the basic assumption of the whole Survey, the real work was done by the stewards of the magnates and a large number of officials and of scribes who had committed to writing all these manorial descriptions in advance of the open county court sessions. Again and again Domesday reports that the county says this, or the Hundred says that, but every now and then we read that 'there was no one to answer (*responderet*) for these lands, but by the men of the county they are valued at £8' (D.B. I, f. 166 b 1): or, as at Woodchester (ibid., f. 164 a 2) 'concerning this manor no one rendered an account, not did any of them (*aliquis eorum*) attend this Survey (*descriptionem*)'. To me, such entries suggest that behind the formal façade of oral procedure, the commissioners relied, in fact, not upon juries, but on individuals with exact knowledge of the facts on each manor, and if so, we must assume that these particulars were already committed to writing when the court met. Thus in court the commissioners systematically reviewed the evidence Hundred by Hundred, while clerks behind the scenes regrouped the information in the manner demanded by the terms of reference, that is personally, by the fee and the 'honour'. But it is only when the formal procedure broke down that we can discover the actual process followed. The text of the Survey is thickly studded with brief summaries of what must have been time-consuming disputes in court, owing to conflict of evidence. Take, for example, this instance in Hampshire (f. 44 b 2):

William de Chernet claims this land saying (*dicens*) that it belongs to the manor of Cerdeford . . . and on this matter he brought forward the testimony of men of substance (*melioribus*) and of old men of the whole county and hundred; and Picot offered in opposition the testimony of villagers and rustics (*villanis et vili plebe*) and reeves (*prepositis*) ready to affirm by oath or by judgement of God (*dei judicium*) that he who held the land was a freeman and could go with his land wherever he wished. But William's witnesses would accept no testimony except that of King Edward until the matter should be settled by the king.

The land in question was only 2½ virgates; and scores of such entries suggest that, amid so much wrangling, the main function of the court sessions must have been to pass 'as read' a detailed record already in writing.[1]

The testimony of juries from every Hundred or Wapentake was therefore a basic element of procedure in every circuit, and served at least three purposes:

1. It was a guarantee that no estates escaped the Survey, and so were omitted.

2. It was an independent check upon the information tendered by the holders of land through their officials, and included always some individual connected with every manor, either the actual holder or someone on his behalf.

[1] See *M.D.B.*, pp. 66–7.

3. It afforded the sanction necessary to gain the acquiescence of the land-holders as to the accuracy and therefore the truth of the detailed Survey.

It was therefore an essential but largely formal part of the Survey, which rested upon written statistics supplied by relatively humble clerks, and entailed immense efforts by what are sometimes called the 'backroom boys' such as still do the real work on modern royal commissions. The purpose of the Survey is clearly set out in the 'terms of reference' as a return of the lands held by tenants-in-chief, who are all named in Domesday Book itself. That this testimony by the Hundred was everywhere committed to writing is unproved, and, on the evidence available, unlikely. Indeed in circuit No. II (Exon) it seems wellnigh certain that it was never written down, for the whole manuscript omits to identify the manors by citing the Hundreds in which they lay. However that may be, a single solitary glimpse of this all-important, but preliminary and largely formal, procedure has come down to us accidentally in the Inquisitio Comitatus Cantabrigiensis, a late manuscript of private provenance, and extraordinarily corrupt, based on early drafts of the returns of three circuits. A penultimate version of the return from circuit No. II still survives in Exon Domesday, and—most revealingly of all—the actual circuit return itself from the *legati* who dealt with East Anglia(No.VII) is now Volume II of Domesday Book.

The making of the circuit returns is a subject as yet only half explored; but the general outline is clear; and the main points about this very complicated process can be summarized as follows:

1. Every circuit, it seems now safe to assume, followed the guide-lines laid down in the terms of reference. The common object was a record, identical in form with the final abbreviation which survives in Volume I of Domesday Book. So each county was separately treated, beginning with a description of the county town, and a numbered

list of those who 'held lands' in it, that is to say, who were tenants-in-chief. Then followed the detailed description of every royal manor in the county, and this record of royal demesne was referred to as the 'breve regis'. Then, in order of precedence, successively the *breve* of each tenant-in-chief, from the highest to the lowest, the humbler tenants, such as thegns or chaplains, being often grouped under a single heading. The numbers of tenants-in-chief varied widely from county to county. In Kent, for example, the numbered list is no more than 13; in Yorkshire it was 29, and in Devonshire 53.

2. All estates held by mesne tenure are recorded under the names of the tenants-in-chief, and the majority of these themselves held some of their lands as sub-tenants of other tenants-in-chief.

3. For two of the circuits, viz. Nos. II and III, we have remains of early drafts of part of the final returns, while for circuit No. VII we have the final return itself, which is now Volume II of Domesday Book. Traces of the circuit returns also remain for circuits I and V among what are called the 'satellite' surveys. For the others we have only the final shortened version in Volume I.

4. On every circuit the initial formal procedure was based on the evidence of sworn jurors from each Hundred or Wapentake, and in the Cambridge circuit (No. III) this was fully recorded in writing. There is no clear evidence that this was done on any other circuit, though it may have been; and the evidence suggests that in the south-west (No. II) and in East Anglia (No. VII) the hundredal testimony appears to have been rearranged as individual *breves* from the start. But the procedure of sworn evidence, technically supposed to have been given verbally by the hundred juries and by the tenants-in-chief, was fundamental since it constituted the legal sanction for any future action taken by the Crown. One of the tenants-in-chief in Little Domesday (Vol. II) actually speaks of the day on which he was '*inbreviatus*'.

5. The circuit *legati*, though nowhere referred to as justices (*justiciarii*), often acted as such. There were endless wrangles which in many cases they settled in court; but in circuit No. VI they added an appendix of *clamores* for Huntingdon, Yorkshire, and Lincolnshire; in East Anglia a similar list of *invasiones*; and in Exon Domesday lists of *terrae occupatae*, which, however, were omitted from the shortened version in Volume I of Domesday.

6. The evidence proves that each circuit return involved more than one preliminary draft, and that someone had to be present in the county court to 'answer for' the details regarding each estate. It also suggests a lively activity out of court, and behind the scenes, devoted to getting the facts down in writing in preparation for the court sittings.

7. Of the geld inquisition (*inquisitio geldi*) which immediately preceded the Survey in 1086 our only evidence comes from the Exon Domesday, and the testimony of Robert, bishop of Hereford. Its object was to discover 'lost hides', that is, estates which had long evaded payment of the geld. Exon Domesday affords clear evidence that the Domesday *legati* made use of its findings in this circuit. An entry in Staffordshire Domesday implies that the levy of a geld was virtually an annual event by the time of the Survey. There had been a collection of geld at 6*s*. on the hide in 1084, and there was certainly another at the same rate in 1086. This was accompanied by a special *inquisitio* designed to secure its full payment, and so complete the Survey of the total national wealth.

IV

DOMESDAY BOOK

A. *Volume I: Great Domesday*

THE two volumes of Domesday Book, though our first public record, are by no means the earliest surviving document emanating from William I's administration. A number of his royal writs still remain, products of his Chancery and sealed with his great seal. The Chancery, however, was itinerant and followed the king, while Domesday, it is safe to assume, was written at Winchester, already the seat of the royal treasury. Who exactly wrote it we do not know, but the character of the writing stamps it as a *curial* or court script written by a highly trained scribe whose employment was with purely business documents. The sole purpose of Domesday was as a work of reference for the king's officials, and so the writing is very severely abbreviated. The only people who used it were well aware that M meant *manerium*, and T.R.E. meant *tempore regis Edwardi*, and so on. At the same time, it is in a *set* hand, not found among the surviving royal writs, though, like them, it is perfectly clear, and highly professional: what in fact we should call today 'a fair copy'. It is written, Mr. Hector tells us, 'in a clear Carolingian minuscule and its headings and displayed matter in rustic capitals'.[1] It was, in short, a great official undertaking intended for perpetual preservation and handy reference.

'This brings us to a problem which Domesday commentators have generally neglected or at least treated

[1] L. C. Hector, *The Handwriting of English Documents*, p. 51.

somewhat casually'.[1] The Survey began after Christmas
1085 and was completed—so far as it *was* completed[2]—
by the death of William I in September 1087. The whole
enterprise, the making of the circuit returns and their
'abbreviation' in Volume I of Domesday, occupied less
than two years. Had it been written in a calligraphic text
hand, such as was employed for costly copies of the Bible
and the works of the Fathers, it would probably have
taken longer, but Mr. Alfred Fairbank, C.B.E.,[3] an
authority on writing and himself an expert scribe, is of
opinion that the job could have been done in a year or so,
which is probably just about the time that must have been
available. More important than the time taken in writing
Volume I is Mr. Fairbank's conviction that the whole
book was written by a single scribe. So far as I am aware,
Mr. Fairbank was the first to assert positively this rather
startling view, with which Mr. Hector's statement quoted
above seems to agree. For myself, I can only say that
having worked with Domesday for more than half a
century, I am of the same opinion. The script is very
individual or, as palaeographers put it, very idiosyncratic,
that is, recognizable at a glance; and whether written big
or small, carefully or hurriedly—for all these variations
can be found in Volume I's 382 folios—there is, *me judice*,
no page or passage which could not have been written by
the same scribe.

The conclusion that the whole of Volume I of Domesday
Book was written by one scribe in a fine, set hand such
as we normally associate with 'a fair copy' is of crucial
importance. For there is ample evidence in its numerous
corrections and marginal additions to prove that it is
not in fact just a mechanical copy, but the actual manuscript in which some high official drastically abbreviated

---

[1] *Domesday Re-Bound* (Public Record Office, 1954), p. 54, a work essential to
Domesday study, the 'bulk of the material' being compiled by Miss D. H.
Gifford.

[2] The existence of Volume II, in fact, proves that it never was quite completed.

[3] *Domesday Re-Bound*, p. 31.

the returns from every circuit, except No. VII, East Anglia. How exactly he went to work can be seen by comparing an entry in Exon Domesday with the shorter version in Volume I. Carl Stephenson[1] illustrates the process by the following typical entry for Somersetshire:

Serlo has a manor (*mansionem*) which is called Lovington and which three thegns, Aelmarus and Siricus and a woman Alfilla, held in parage (*pariter*) on the day King Edward was alive and dead. It rendered geld (*reddidit gildum*) for 6 hides. Those can be cultivated by (*possunt arare*) 8 plows. Of the aforesaid hides Aelmarus had 4 hides and Siricus 1 and Alfilla another hide. These lands Serlo holds as a manor. Of them Serlo has 3 hides minus 5 acres, and 2 plows in demesne; and the villeins [have] 2 hides and 5 acres, and 6 plows. And [there are] 8 villeins and 9 bordars and 2 slaves; and 16 beasts (*animalia*) and 1 riding-horse and 11 swine and 80 sheep; and a mill that renders 10s. annually; and a wood 4 furlongs in length and 2 in breadth; and 40 acres of meadow. And it is worth 100s. annually, and when Serlo received it 6l.

In Volume I this appears as follows:

Serlo himself holds Lovington. Three thegns held it T.R.E. as three manors and it gelded (*geldabat*) for 6 hides. There is land for 8 plows. In demesne there are 2 plows, and [there are] 2 slaves and 8 villeins and 9 bordars with 6 plows. In it a mill renders 10s., and [there are] 40 acres of meadow; [also] a wood 4 furlongs in length and 2 furlongs in breadth. Previously [it was worth] 6l.; now 100s.

The condensation upon which the compiler of Volume I was intent was obtained by discarding some of the longer formulas in favour of briefer ones, omission of repetitious phrases and of much detailed information, including the names of the three thegns, the statement that they held in parage, the distribution among them of the six hides, the division of the six hides between Serlo and his villeins, and the statistics about livestock.

This entry, typical, of thousands, reveals the mind of the compiler. He is set to produce the shortest possible

---

[1] *Medieval Institutions*, p. 189.

record of the basic facts, discarding all that is merely
ephemeral. Such an epitome, deliberately made with an
eye to the future, is unique among our public records, and
a supreme example of the fiercely practical Norman
genius. All but the essential was ruthlessly discarded.
Stephenson in quoting this example speaks of the 'compilers' of Domesday Book, but the responsibility for such
an operation could hardly have been shared. Only some
high and trusted official could be allowed to abandon so
much of the hardly garnered information. The more we
study Volume I, the stronger is the impression of a single
mind at work.

Recent research has thrown new light upon Samson,
a royal chaplain successively of William I and William II,
who was promoted to the bishopric of Worcester in 1096
and lived until 1112. Archbishop Lanfranc seems to have
corresponded with him regarding the Survey of 1086, and
Samson's own estates are oddly treated in Domesday
Book. We also find in Heming's cartulary, which was
compiled at Worcester during his pontificate, certain
unique Domesday documents. Finally and convincingly
the late Mr. Welldon Finn showed that the scribe of
Volume I wrote at least two entries (couched in the final
terms of Vol. I) in Exon Domesday itself.[1] All this points
towards Samson as the likely compiler of Volume I, 'the
man behind the Survey'. It is no more than a hypothesis,
like so much in Domesday matters, but a very likely one
which might yet be clinched by further examination.[2]
Samson was a colourful figure, a bishop of the old school
and a man of the world, who clearly was in the confidence
of both William I and William II. William of Malmesbury gossips about him in his *Gesta Pontificum*. If indeed
he was the compiler of Domesday, we still cannot be

---

[1] 'The Evolution of Successive Versions of the Domesday Survey', *E.H.R.*,
1951, p. 561.
[2] V. H. Galbraith, 'Notes on the Career of Samson, bishop of Worcester
1096–1112', *E.H.R.*, 1967, p. 86.

quite certain that he was the scribe. He seems to have come from Bayeux, and so important a person could have had his own expert writer, though I think it unlikely.[1] However that may be, all recent students of Domesday agree that behind the immense task of epitomizing seven, or more, circuit returns drawn up in the same manner as Volume I itself, we can trace the workings of a single mind imposing a set, if rough, pattern on very diverse materials; for manners, customs, terminology, and even hidage assessment varied widely from county to county, and even more widely from region to region. The north, in particular, with its carucates, wapentakes, bovates, etc., was basically different from the south of England, with its hides and its Hundreds. The measurements of woodland varied a lot and the pannage for swine was variously computed. The compiler had to make do with the material sent to him, and to the last there remained many blank spaces in Volume I which reflect the failure of the local *legati* to extract the exact figures. But inconsistencies in arrangement were carefully made good, so that the numbered lists of tenants-in-chief which occupy the first page of each county are—with one solitary exception[2] which proves the rule—set out in strict order of precedence, viz. the king, archbishops, bishops, abbots, earls, barons, and so on, down the social scale. Similarly, where the name of a mesne tenant, as in Yorkshire,[3] has inadvertently crept into the initial county list of tenants, the whole of his manors have been redistributed by the compiler among the various tenants-in-chief from whom he held them.

These numbered lists of tenants-in-chief, which serve as an index to the whole county return, throw light, when carefully examined, on the actual procedure of the compiler

[1] See *M.D.B.*, p. 203, where I was more positive about this than I am now. Contrariwise, I am now entirely convinced that the whole volume was written by a single scribe.

[2] Nottinghamshire.

[3] The abbot of St. Mary's, York.

of Great Domesday. He began by copying from the circuit return before him the prefatory list of 'holders of land', and then, turning over, got down to the task of abbreviating the record of each tenant, beginning with the king's land (*Terra Regis*) numbered I. Having the full record before him, he had no need to turn back again to his numbered list, and proceeded to correct errors and to make such editorial changes as were required. Only when this was completed was it necessary to consult the circuit index again in order to 'rubricate', that is to number in red paint, his own preliminary index in Volume I, and then to rubricate the full entry of each tenant or holder. In some counties, it is found, that he had so altered the grouping and titles in the new, shorter, text that the red numbers had to be 'fudged' in order to correspond with the text that followed. It was Eyton who first called attention to this in regard to Somerset and Dorset.[1] In these counties, the discrepancies are glaring, but a minute examination shows that a *perfect* correspondence between the prefatory list in Volume I and the text that follows it was nowhere achieved. The differences are often trifling, but they are there and prove to demonstration that the circuit returns were identical in form (though much more lengthy) with the abbreviated record in Great Domesday. This conclusion harmonizes with the testimony of Little Domesday, which in origin was just one of the circuit returns. That volume was the 'fair copy' made for return to Winchester, and the scribe had to refer back to his preliminary list on f. 1 to make sure that his main text followed his index exactly. And it does, for the scribe or rather scribes, for there were many, on ff. 9, 17, and 372 copied from the preliminary index the next group of fees to be successively dealt with in the text, and, when entered, simply crossed out these aids to memory. Trifling as these minutiae are in themselves, they are precious evidence such as only original manuscripts can

---

[1] *Key to Domesday: Dorset*, p. 74. Cf. *M.D.B.*, p. 193.

supply regarding the exact procedure followed by the scribes.

For the historical student, anxious to relate the text of Domesday to the feudal history of the late eleventh century, the Introductions to the Domesday texts included in the *Victoria County Histories* supply an elaborate and most valuable commentary. No other country can compare with England in the wealth of precise factual knowledge Domesday provides for the study of strictly contemporary feudalism. The subject is well-nigh endless, and may be here illustrated by a single example of the problems faced by the compilers of the Survey regarding Roger of Poitou.

Roger of Poitou,[1] Rogerus Pictavensis, appears in both volumes of Domesday Book as a large landowner in many counties. There is, however, a difficulty: for in some of them the lands, though fully described, are said to be now in the king's hand. Thus in Essex his name is no. 46 in the prefatory table of tenants, and a full description of his lands is headed *Terra Rogeri Pictavensis*. In Suffolk also he is entered as a normal tenant, and in Vol. I similarly he appears in Nottinghamshire, and Lincolnshire, and in Hampshire (in the margin) as holding a single manor. Against this we have to set the counties of Chester (the lands between the Ribble and the Mersey), Yorkshire, Derbyshire, and (in Little Domesday) Norfolk, where his lands are said to be in the king's hand. Moreover, there are signs of uncertainty and hesitation in these shires. In Yorkshire, for instance, his name does not appear in the prefatory table of tenants, but a full description of his lands is added on a blank leaf at the end of the county (f. 332). In Norfolk his name appears in the table, but the list of his lands is headed *Terre que fuerunt Rogeri Pictavensis* (f. 243 a). Finally, in Derbyshire he is in the table, and his lands are described as *Terra Rogeri Pictavensis*, but at the end of the fee is added 'Has terras habebat Rogerus Pictavensis, modo sunt in manu regis' (f. 273 b 1).

These conflicting entries, which still baffle Roger's biographers, at least throw light on the making of the Survey. They seem to show that Roger's lands were taken into the king's hands at a later date in

---

[1] *M.D.B.*, pp. 187–8.

the year 1086, when the original returns were everywhere all but completed. In some cases the text of a particular county was finished before the news reached the local commissioners; in others it arrived just in time to be noted. They also prove that Little Domesday (which we know was made in 1086) is contemporary with the original returns of the circuits abbreviated in Vol. I. More generally we can, I think, confidently attribute Exon and the two volumes of Domesday Book to William I's reign, and no later, since Roger rose very quickly to such high favour with his successor, that no such confusion would later have been possible.

This was written in 1962. I repeat it here, since the old fallacy that all or any of our three original manuscripts were compiled *after* the reign of William I still dies hard. The story of Roger of Poitou in Domesday vividly describes for us contemporary history in the making.

There is no need here to describe in detail the make-up of Great Domesday, which is minutely analysed in *Domesday Re-bound* (1954); but some points call for notice. Neither the circuit returns nor, of course, Domesday itself were cast in the form of Rolls, which belong to a later age. These imaginary 'Rolls' [*Rotuli*] were given currency by Ellis in his *Introduction to Domesday* (1833) and misled his successors for a century. The Normans dealt in quaternions, that is quires or booklets of eight leaves, or sixteen pages. Little Domesday being a 'fair copy' or at least a final draft of the circuit return was written straight through as a single book, and has only five inserted leaves in 450 folios. In Great Domesday, on the other hand, each county was made up as a separate booklet, filling one or more complete quires according to size.[1] Until, somewhat later, they were bound up to form a single book, they seem to have been used separately, and it is noteworthy that the 'circuit order' was abandoned when this was done. The unit in Domesday is the county, and their grouping into circuits a mere administrative

---

[1] There are some interesting exceptions. See *M.D.B.*, pp. 199 ff., and *Domesday Re-Bound*, Appendices.

device adopted to get the job done quickly As there is still uncertainty regarding the number of circuits and their composition, we can only guess at the reasons which prompted the order in which the counties appear in Domesday. It begins, and no doubt was meant to begin, with Kent followed by a 'band', as it were, of the southern counties running from east to west. A second 'band' begins with Middlesex and works westward to Hereford: then a third from Cambridge to Cheshire, which bends back to include Derby and Nottingham. The volume ends with Lincolnshire and Yorkshire which—even in Domesday Book—are made up to form a single separate booklet. Had Little Domesday been abbreviated and added, Essex would probably have preceded Middlesex, and Norfolk and Suffolk preceded Cambridge.

One last question remains regarding the compilation of Great Domesday. Assuming, as we have done, that the whole volume was written by a single scribe, is there any means of deciding in what order of counties he epitomized the circuit returns? Some light is thrown on this matter by the remarkable evidence in *Domesday Re-Bound* regarding what is there described as the 'horizontal rulings' of the manuscript, that is the number of lines of writing on each page. In so splendid a volume one would expect the number to remain constant, and the writing of one size. Actually, there is wide variation, and the editors of *Domesday Re-Bound* found the reason for it in the scribe's growing sense of urgency to complete his task, even at the cost of some lowering of standards. Their results may be summarized as follows:

The compiler seems to have begun in a large careful hand, allowing only 44 lines to the page. This he employed in dealing with the circuit which included Middlesex, Hertford, Buckingham, Cambridge, and Bedford; and so continued with circuit no. VI, through Huntingdon, Nottingham, Derby, and Lincolnshire. In Yorkshire we find the number of lines to the page increased to nearly 50, and since we presume that the commissioners worked outwards (and in this case northwards), the change took place while he was abbreviating the last county in his local return. Next, perhaps, he turned to abbreviate the return of the first circuit— Kent, Surrey, Sussex, Hampshire, and Berkshire, where we find consistently 50 lines to the page. All this suggests that the compiler was feeling the necessity for compression by getting more on the page, and in his abbreviation of circuit no. IV, Oxford, Leicester, Northampton, the number of lines to the page runs in places to nearly 60. Finally, and most strangely, in circuit no. II, that of the south-western counties, and V, the Welsh border, the compiler eventually ceased to rule any lines at all. This change we might attribute to laziness or carelessness, but this in fact is not the impression left by the writing for these counties, which is still most competently done. Rather, the change seems due to haste, haste to get the job finished and therefore at all costs to compress within the space allotted the shortened version of his material. This is especially noticeable in the south-western circuit, and a glance at the facsimile of the first folio for Wiltshire, for example, shows that the compiler, forced to get into his page more than it would hold, actually ignored the lines he had ruled across it. There are no less than thirteen gatherings which are not ruled at all. They comprise much of the south-western counties and all of those on the Welsh border, and we can hardly doubt both that they were the last written and that they are left unruled to expedite the completion of the book. By ignoring the ruled page an entry could be written in as large or as small a script as there was room for, and to these striking variations in the size and carefulness of the script is chiefly due the tendency of paleographers to presume a number of different scribes. The key to the problem lies in the fact that the scribe was abbreviating a much larger original, also arranged by counties, and had to estimate before he began the size of the quire he needed, so that each county section of his abbreviation should form a separate, self-contained booklet.[1]

B. *Volume II: Little Domesday*

Domesday Book, Volume II, Little Domesday, is, in its way, as unique as Volume I, Great Domesday, since it is the actual circuit return (No. VII) drawn up by the *legati* somewhere in East Anglia and returned to Winchester,

[1] *M.D.B.,* pp. 203–4.

but never abbreviated, and so never included in Volume I. Had this been done, it would itself have long since disappeared, and the modern historian would have been much less well informed concerning the most populous and prosperous region in all England. In Little Domesday we can trace the way in which the *legati* struggled against peculiar difficulties to comply with the requirements of the 'terms of reference' under which they acted. The result is a volume, drawn up in the same form as Volume I, but on a far more generous scale; for it contains details about the stock on the demesne, or home farm of each manor, details about population both in 1066 and 1086, and—most exciting of all—a mass of evidence regarding the actual procedure in court, such as is nowhere found in Volume I. This is of great importance, for it shows how firmly the procedure of the *legati* was based upon the evidence of the hundredal juries, whose testimony far exceeds that of the county. In Norfolk, for example, the 'men of the Hundred' testify (*testantur*) or say (*dicunt*) something on more than fifty occasions, while the evidence of the county is nowhere mentioned. Much the same is true of Suffolk, while in Essex the county testifies half a dozen times, and the Hundred about forty. To all this we must add the many instances of testimony from sheriffs and individual barons, each instance generally involving a conflict of evidence in court. The final impression is of mixed wonder and admiration that this vast waste of statistics was ever completed at all. For nowhere else in England were there so many humble 'freemen' and 'socmen', who are here seen so stubbornly claiming their rights.

On the other hand, it is most unlikely that any written document of the testimony of the hundredal juries—such as that for Cambridgeshire (in the I.C.C.)—was ever made in East Anglia; for Volume II constantly refers to each tenant-in-chief's lands as forming a separate 'breve' or schedule, and it is here that Robert Malet

(f. 276 b) mentions the 'day on which he was listed' (*inbreviatus*). There are, too, repeated cross-references from one baron's *breve* to another. So from the very beginning the *legati* seem to have been thinking of a feudal return arranged under the names of the king (who also has his 'breve') and of each tenant-in-chief. And this, of course, is implicit in the terms of reference under which the *legati* acted.

A single instance may serve to illustrate the wealth of incidental information supplied by Little Domesday. It relates to the manor of Hoxne, the site of the bishopric of Suffolk (f. 379 a). Translated, it reads:

> In this manor there was a market in the time of King Edward, and after King William arrived; and it used to sit (*sedebat*) on Saturday; and William Malet made his castle at Eye; and on the same day that there was a market in the bishop's manor, William Malet set up (*fecit*) another market in his castle, and the bishop's market was so worsened (*peioratum*) as to be worth very little (*parum*); and now it meets on Friday. But the market at Eye meets on Saturday. William Malet holds it by the King's gift.

When one turns from the printed text to the manuscript it is at once seen to present a violent contrast to Volume I. This struck Round, who wrote,[1]

> I have never seen any attempt at a real explanation of the great difference both in scope and in excellence between the two volumes, or indeed any reason given why the Eastern counties should have had a volume to themselves. For a full appreciation of the contrast presented by the two volumes, the originals ought to be examined. Such differences as that the leaves of one are half as large again as those of the other, and that the former is drawn up in double, but the latter in single column, dwarf the comparatively minor contrasts of material and handwriting. So too the fulness of the details in the second volume obscure the fact of its workmanship being greatly inferior to that of the first.

Here we trace the 'upward anguish' of historical research in England. In 1895 it was a new idea to look at the

[1] *F.E.*, p. 140.

'original MS.', while the differences of the script between the two volumes were only 'minor contrasts'.[1] By 1954 *Domesday Re-Bound* had greatly advanced the problem by its immense insistence upon the differences between the two in script, style, material (one calf skin, the other sheepskin), pigment employed by the rubricator, the headings, and the gatherings. Of these, the arch-difference lies in the writing. In place of a volume written in splendid, expert curial script, Volume II is the work of many non-curial penmen, writing—with greatly varying skill—the ordinary minuscules found in monastic writings of the time. The conclusion is forced upon us that the two books are of wholly different provenance: and since Volume I was made at Winchester, Volume II was not. 'The entries of the Little Domesday Book', writes Professor Darby,[2] 'are more cumbrous and untidy than those of the main Domesday Book. They give the impression of being more hastily compiled.' He is quite right. They were *very* hastily compiled indeed, and a close analysis of the quires provides the final link in the evidence that Volume II was itself the local circuit return. For, as explained above (p. 20), Volume II is no more than a very hasty fair copy of an earlier draft and is, as we should expect, full of errors, not the least of which is the omission of Burgh Apton,[3] which must have been in the exemplar. This conclusion is further supported by the list of holders of land in Norfolk (f. 109), where lay barons' names precede those of bishops and abbots, which the Winchester abbreviator would certainly have corrected had the volume emanated from there. And for good measure it should also be mentioned that the scribes

---

[1] From this misunderstanding of the MS., Round suggested that Vol. II was 'a first attempt at the codification of the returns' which he envisaged as a huge collection of hundred rolls. Many years later he claimed in the *V.C.H. Essex*, vol. i, p. 413, to have proved this hypothesis regarding Little Domesday, the nature of which had completely eluded him. Cf. below, p. 150.

[2] *Domesday Geography of Eastern England*, p. 97.

[3] From f. 214 b.

of Volume II, hastily copying their material, often make
use of the first person (e.g. *ut superius diximus*, 'as we said
above'), unconsciously retaining the direct speech of
their source. In the King's *breve* for Essex (f. 2 b) the
scribe even writes 'Afterwards we recovered (*recuperavi-
mus*) a hide which one of Harold's socmen held in the
time of King Edward.'

The Victorians, it may here be repeated, were fasci-
nated by the collection of the geld in which they seemed
to see the early existence of the Direct Taxation which
was such a feature of the nineteenth century. They all
agreed that the primary motive of the whole Survey was
to reassess this ancient 'custom' on a 'new, fair and equitable basis'. However we look at it, this was a hopeless
anachronism and one that could have been corrected even
then from Little Domesday. For in East Anglia geld
collection was arranged on a system unique in all England.
The villages there were elaborately grouped in a system
of 'leets', each village paying so much for every pound
paid by the Hundred. Geld could therefore only have
been reassessed on the basis of these 'leets', which Volume
II fails to distinguish. Nor is their arrangement recorded
anywhere until a century later, and then only for the lands
of the Abbey of St. Edmund at Bury.[1] But, all this apart,
we are now compelled by Robert of Hereford's testimony
(above, p. 22) to conclude that the Domesday Survey was
immediately preceded by an *inquisitio geldi*, the object of
which was to discover 'non-paying hides'. A 6-shilling
geld was certainly collected in the year 1086 on the basis
of this Inquest, but it had no direct connnection with the
Survey. To have carried out this immense Survey merely
or even chiefly in order to reassess the geld would then
have been, as it were, to use a steam hammer to crack an
egg. The true nature of Norman finance is first disclosed
to us in the Pipe Rolls of which the earliest is that of 31

---

[1] See R. H. C. Davis (ed.), *The Kalendar of Abbot Samson* (R. Hist. Soc.,
Camden Third Series, 1954).

Henry I (1129–30), which contains the record of a geld at 2 shillings on the hide; but this was no more than an item in an intricate nexus of feudal finance. Its chief features, which certainly reach back to William I's reign, can be summarized as follows:

1. Each county owed an annual 'farm' to the Crown based upon its rents and rights of the royal demesne, and the profits of justice.

2. This revenue fluctuated from year to year, as estates escheated to the Crown by the death of tenants-in-chief either without heirs or by reason of rebellion.

3. From every tenant-in-chief the Crown took 'a relief' from the heir to a barony on his father's death, or sold to another baron the 'wardship' of an heir under age. The Crown also exacted a payment on the marriage of an heiress; and finally, from time to time, took an 'aid' or a 'scutage' from the king's tenants-in-chief.

4. The Crown received the revenues of vacant bishoprics and abbacies.

5. A very large amount came from 'fines' of all kinds paid by tenants-in-chief either for special privileges or for regaining the king's favour after a quarrel.

6. In the early twelfth-century 'geld', an immemorial 'custom', was collected annually, and it is safe to say that by the close of William I's reign geld was already thought of as if not an annual occurrence one collected at the discretion of the Crown. But it was hedged about by many personal exemptions from payment and the total exemption of 'demesne' lands: and, when the figures are known in the twelfth century, brought in only about £3,000 in any one year.

The purpose of the Survey was directed towards the first five of these categories. But it was preceded by a special geld inquest in the same year. The Survey wrung from the tenants-in-chief for the first time a comprehensive acknowledgement of their individual assets, as well as informing the Crown of the full value of royal demesne.

It was thus essentially a record in a feudal world of the wealth of tenants-in-chief, whose earldoms and baronies were made up of estates generally spread over a number of counties. The ancient administrative and financial system of counties and Hundreds in England thus provided the only practical way of measuring the wealth of an essentially new feudal order based on the homage of tenants-in-chief—earls, barons, and other lesser figures—owing knight service to the Crown, and all the other incidents of tenure mentioned above. Little Domesday and Exon Domesday alone set before us in minute detail the extraordinary complexities of individual, humble tenure on which landed wealth depended. In Great Domesday most of this was sacrificed, as ephemeral, in favour of a manageable summary.

One other question is raised by the survival of Little Domesday: Were the *legati* who drew it up aware that the central government had decided to epitomize their findings? The meticulous manner in which they strove to record the age-long confusions of land-holding in East Anglia rather suggests that each circuit thought of its return as the final record. The answer to this question is, perhaps, supplied by the rubrication of the volume. In Volume II each county begins with a list of the tenants-in-chief whose 'fees' are afterwards summarized in it. At some time after its completion the book was rubricated in red paint, that is to say, the prefatory list of tenants was numbered on f. 1—in Essex I–LXXXVIII, in Norfolk I–LXVI, and in Suffolk I–LXXVI; and these red numbers inserted in the margin at the beginning of each fee. Exactly the same procedure was followed in Great Domesday, where we have already seen that in no single county does this prefatory list entirely correspond with the text that follows. In Little Domesday on the other hand, the prefatory list of tenants-in-chief agrees exactly with the text that follows, and from time to time the scribes have listed and later crossed out in the margins the next group of fees to be entered. But a glance at these prefatory lists in Little Domesday suggests that the scribes had not allowed proper space for the insertion of the rubricated numbers. It seems most likely then that the whole of the rubrication of Volume II was added as an afterthought when Volume II was, *faute de mieux*, promoted to rank with Volume I as part of the final Domesday: that, in short, they were making the best of a bad job.[1] Indeed, it is quite possible that for Volume II the central authorities despaired of making a workable epitome, when they received this maze of statistics, and decided that they would have to 'make do' with it by adding a crude rubrication to harmonize with Volume I. This possibility agrees with the rubricated colophon on the last folio, identifying the volume with the rest of the Survey, where they were careful to add that a like Survey was carried out in all the other English counties.

One last feature seems to show that Volume II was made in the provinces, and not at Winchester. The record of the towns, and some of them were considerable, is not in Little Domesday put at the head of the county, but set out in full in the course of the text in accordance with the hundredal sequence invariably pursued in this volume.[2] Thus in East Anglia, as elsewhere, the *legati* collected from a jury of each Hundred a minute description of every estate in it. But this was no more than a first step, and we have no knowledge of any written record in this circuit drawn up on the lines of the I.C.C. These verdicts of the Hundreds must have been checked against the facts of tenure submitted by the land stewards of the earls, barons, and other tenants-in-chief, and this information must have been laboriously tendered to the *legati* behind the scenes or at least out of court, where so much time was

---

[1] For example, in Norfolk (f. 273) the rubricator inadvertently omitted to paint a red ten—X—in the margin, where the description of the fee of Roger Bigot begins. Nor is there any other rubrication on this page. He seems simply to have turned over two pages by mistake.

[2] See below, p. 155.

clearly consumed in trying to harmonize conflicting testimony. It is possible, and indeed not unlikely, that the *legati* had already before them the *breve* or schedule of each great landowner when the hundred juries delivered their verdicts in open court.

c. *Exon Domesday*

Though not technically a 'public' record, since it has never been in the custody of the Crown, Exon Domesday is as much an 'original' of the Domesday Survey as Volumes I and II. On these three manuscripts must depend our whole picture of the Survey. Obvious as this is, the point needs to be stressed, since by an accident of history, the evidence of Exon has been veiled in a cloud of uncertainty and suspicion, and so virtually ignored until the middle of this century. The explanation of this critical aberration goes back to an error of the Revd. R. W. Eyton, who, as mentioned above,[1] identified the geld accounts it contains as those of the 1084 collection mentioned in the Anglo-Saxon Chronicle. It was an unfortunate error, made by a fine scholar who did pioneer work on Exon, in defence of a wrong-headed theory of the 'fiscal' hide. J. H. Round dealt faithfully with the 'fiscal' hide, but clung, calamitously, to the theory that the Domesday *legati* in 1086 were still using the geld records of 1084. Round's study of the I.C.C. had already suggested to him that the original returns to Winchester were a vast array of 'Hundred Rolls', which carefully identified every manor according to the Hundred in which it was situated. But this theory is irreconcilable with Exon Domesday, in which the manors are already grouped, county by county, under the names of the tenants-in-chief, but *without any reference to the Hundreds in which they lay*. Encouraged by Eyton's removal of the geld accounts from the year 1086, Round virtually rules out Exon from his writings.

[1] p. 20.

In the pedigree of Domesday manuscripts in *Feudal England*[1] he ostentatiously omitted Exon Domesday, by putting it in a footnote, and many years later flatly asserted that its composition and character were inexplicable. Writing of Somerset Domesday in the *Victoria County History*, he concluded his long Introduction with these words:[2] 'It is greatly to be hoped that the "Exon" Book will some day receive at the hands of a trained scholar the critical treatment of which it stands in need and which may yet reveal its character and its object.' This was turning the blind eye to the telescope with a vengeance, and the 'so-called Exon Domesday' was henceforth relegated to footnotes by his followers. In the Index to *Domesday Book and Beyond*, Maitland, though, like Round himself, making full use of its contents, assigned to Exon only a single reference. However excusable in the nineteenth century, the last defence of Round's position was breached by the publication in 1907 of Robert of Hereford's testimony, which speaks of the many calamities arising from the collection of the king's money (*ex congregatione regalis pecuniae*) in 1086.[3] In the last thirty years research has dispelled the 'mystery' of Exon Domesday. But so much has to be said about a view which had such distinguished sponsors, if only in the interests of Domesday bibliography.[4] Nor can the student assume that this total misapprehension of both the procedure and purpose of the Survey is altogether a thing of the past. On all sides there is still evidence of uncertainty regarding the procedure followed by the circuit *legati*. It is still

---

[1] *F.E.*, p. 146.

[2] *V.C.H. Somerset*, vol. i, p. 432. Round's verdict has lately been repeated by Professor Darlington in the *V.C.H. Wiltshire*, vol. ii, p. 44 (1955): 'a more intensive study of the Exon Domesday than has yet been attempted is needed before the relationship of their two texts can be determined'. And see p. 17 n. 2 above.

[3] Above, pp. 22–5.

[4] See 'The Making of Domesday Book', *E.H.R.*, 1942, and 'The Date of the Geld Rolls in Exon Domesday', *E.H.R.*, 1950, both by the present writer; also J. F. A. Mason, 'The Date of the Geld Rolls', *E.H.R.*, 1954. All this evidence was summarized in *M.D.B.*

found, for example, not only in the Introductions to the Domesday sections of the *Victoria County History*, more especially those dealing with the south-western counties; in Darby's *Domesday Geography;* in *Domesday Re-Bound* (1954); and of course in most, but not all, textbooks. The best available introduction today is the late Mr. Welldon Finn's *Liber Exoniensis* (1964).[1]

The bare facts regarding Exon Domesday are set out above (p. 21); but it demands a closer scrutiny here because it is our solitary example of a circuit return of which we also have the shortened version in Great Domesday. In Exon alone can the student see both what the compiler of Volume I did and how he did it; and for the first time study the text in facsimile. In doing so, it has to be borne in mind that, large as Exon is, it is only a fragment of the full circuit return, and that we can never hope to discover the original make-up of the volume or, more precisely, of the quaternions of which it consisted. As we have it today, the contents are so muddled that I print below a short summary of its contents made for private use when working on it.[2] By reference to this list certain basic facts are instantly brought home to us:

1. It is concerned with the findings of the *legati* in all the five counties of the south-western circuit.

2. Though there is evidence in it of an initial procedure by hundredal juries, the information has already been rearranged under the fees of the tenants-in-chief in each county.

3. Nowhere in it is any effort made to identify the

---

[1] The book is based upon a searching collation of the Domesday text with that of Exon, and the author's conclusion is thus summarized (p. 5): 'For anyone still unwilling to accept the relationship, the study of Baring's exposition [*E.H.R.*, 1912] and the two Domesdays themselves should prove conclusive. The Exchequer text contains very little information absent from the surviving Exeter version, and the few material differences between them are explicable because the Exchequer clerks worked from a slightly supplemented and occasionally corrected copy of the surviving text.'

[2] Appendix.

Hundreds in which individual manors or estates lay; and we owe a great deal to Eyton who first attempted to arrange the material under the various Hundreds. This fact, though it does not itself prove, yet makes it highly unlikely, that any such written record of the hundred evidence as preserved for us by the I.C.C. for Cambridge-shire was ever made by the south-western *legati*. Rather, it suggests that from the beginning the *legati* registered, county by county, each estate under the name of the relevant tenant-in-chief without further identification.

4. Mixed up with the Survey records we have the accounts of the geld paid in 1086, as a result of a separate *inquisitio geldi*, a sworn inquest, in the same year. Ellis in his Introduction to the printed text of Exon had correctly stated that this geld was collected at the time of the Survey and was connected with it. The geld 'inquest' of 1086 is therefore the true starting-point for further inquiry into Exon Domesday, and though there remains some doubt about the names of the *legati* who carried out this pre-liminary inquest, we find in Exon the still unfinished accounts of the collectors of this geld. We cannot be certain why they are there, but their presence seems to justify two inferences. First, that by this date geld collec-tion had once more become an annual or nearly annual event,[1] and though the government must have had records of its actual collection in the past, they seized the oppor-tunity provided by the Survey of 1086 to discover by a limited geld inquest the many 'lost hides' which had for many years escaped taxation. This is proved by the fact that the Survey embodies the obligation of these long 'lost hides'. Secondly, these tax accounts must have proved invaluable to the *legati* as a means of locating the Hundred in which each manor or *mansio* lay. What we still do not know is why the south-western circuit *legati* failed to record the geographical situation of each manor when arranging their return. It looks very much as

[1] Above, p. 61.

though it was a sad blunder on their part. However that may be, it proved irremediable, for in Volume I, Great Domesday, these five counties alone in the whole of England lack any reference to the Hundreds. Their omission is the final proof that the circuit returns were drawn up exactly as we find them in their epitomized form in Domesday; and equally the final proof that Great Domesday was made from them at Winchester, where the compiler could do no more than abbreviate the returns as made to them. And so, Exon, so long ignored by Domesday scholars, is found to be the crucial link in the chain of proof advanced regarding the composition of Domesday.

That the south-western *legati* interpreted their terms of reference as a return of royal demesne and of baronial fees from the outset is further brought out by some valuable, extraneous documents in Exon which show its compilers attempting to record the total fees in all five counties held by some of the tenants-in-chief. These would repay further study, and are reminiscent of other similar documents in the I.C.C. Together they suggest that in every circuit the *legati* assumed that their circuit return was to be the final record of the Survey. The stroke of genius at headquarters which sacrificed so much detail by bringing the unwieldy totality of the returns to a single, however large, volume may well have been unknown and unsuspected by them. Some such view is almost demanded by the remarkable fact that Great Domesday is demonstrably the work of a single high official, whether or not he was himself the scribe, who carried the final responsibility of this minimizing operation undertaken in the interests of future administrative efficiency.

The precise way in which the abbreviator both condensed the leisurely formulas of the south-western circuit return and selected from the wealth of detail it contained the essential and enduring statistics for perpetual preservation is illustrated above.[1] From it we get a vivid picture

[1] p. 49.

of the regional differences in 'diction', as Ellis described it, between the terms used at Winchester and those of the south-west. From the list he prints one may take a few examples:

Exchequer Domesday	*Exon Survey*
acra	agra
geldabat	reddidit gildum
manerium	mansio
nummi	
pastura	pascua
sylva	nemusculum
T.R.E.	die qua rex E. fuit vivus et mortuus

There are also some significant differences in the grouping of some of the minor tenants-in-chief, of which the most curious is a class of 'French thegns'[1] in Somerset who in Great Domesday appear more correctly as 'King's thegns'. Exon also reveals that certain landowners were first described as tenants-in-chief and later discovered to be, in fact, mesne or under-tenants. One of these was Samson, the king's chaplain, who, as I have suggested above,[2] may well have been the man responsible for compiling Domesday, Volume I. Samson held a *mansionem* (manor) called Templecombe which is minutely described on p. 432 of Exon under the heading 'French Thegns in Somerset'. In Volume I of Domesday he appears *correctly* as no more than the sub-tenant of Odo, bishop of Bayeux, and it is reasonable to suppose that this alteration had already been made in the final circuit return to Winchester which was copied, with such amendments, from Exon. Seen alone, this is a small matter, however interesting; but it takes on a higher significance from Mr. Welldon Finn's discovery that in the surviving 500

---

[1] It may be that Professor Douglas has provided us with a clue to this curious blunder: see *Feudal Documents from the Abbey of Bury St. Edmunds* (1932), p. xciii n. 1.　　　　　　　　　　　　　　　　　　　　　　[2] p. 50.

folios of Exon, all written in non-curial hands, there are just two entries written by the same scribe as wrote the whole of Great Domesday.[1] This not only shows Exon was written in 1086, but also suggests the possibility (along with other evidence) that the compiler of the final epitome in Volume I was no other than Samson himself. These entries, though already here abbreviated, as we find them in Volume I, vary slightly in wording and suggest that the south-western *legati* had sought assistance from Winchester before they made their return. There is other evidence that the south-western *legati* made heavy weather over their task, and very probably because they failed to preserve the hundredal locations of the villages during the initial procedure used throughout England of a systematic submission of the facts by hundred juries.

There is a great deal of other extraneous matter in Exon which still bristles with unanswered problems. There are, for example, the long lists of *Terrae Occupatae*,[2] which have no exact counterpart in the text of Great Domesday; and the special attention given to the Abbey of Tavistock, which in Vinogradoff's[3] perverse opinion showed 'that the Exon copy of Domesday had been written for the use of the Abbey of Tavistock, or, at any rate, by scribes prejudiced in its favour, and this at a time when all the operations connected with the Survey had come to a close'. There is also the remote possibility, discussed by Welldon Finn, that Volume I of Domesday was not written at a single place, but in several provincial centres.[4] Other problems surround the unusual terms used in Exon, such as *mansiones de comitatu* and *dominicatus regis ad regnum pertinens*,[5] and the place-names of the Domesday

---

[1] See *E.H.R.*, 1951, pp. 561 ff., for article and facsimiles of the two entries, and *M.D.B.*, p. 109.

[2] Robert S. Hoyt, 'The Terrae Occupatae of Cornwall and the Exon Domesday', *Traditio*, vol. ix, 1953.

[3] *English Society in the Eleventh Century*, p. 228. Cf. H. P. R. Finberg, *E.H.R.*, 1951, p. 121.   [4] *Liber Exoniensis* (1964), p. 150.

[5] Hoyt, *The Royal Demesne*, 1066–1272 (1950), pp. 15, 16.

manuscripts.[1] Periodical publications on such details are endless and rapidly increasing; and the moral of all this activity is that whatever is written today will to some degree be invalidated by later scholars. The single aim of an *Introduction* to Domesday is to charter the progress so far made in recovering the actual broad procedure followed, though with much variation, by all the circuits, and for this the only unexceptionable evidence is that of our three surviving original manuscripts of the Survey. The most pressing problems today surround the fuller interpretation of the I.C.C., the I.E.,[2] and Exon Domesday itself; and the difficulty here lies in the fact that the I.C.C. and I.E. are only partial transcripts, made a century later, of the original circuit returns before they were finalized. The deeper we probe, the more strongly the evidence indicates the disappearance of a quantity of early drafts, themselves accompanied by a feverish collection of data out of court, and so behind the scenes. To contemporaries, who realized the difficulties, the mere making of the Survey was an administrative miracle, the extraordinary complexities of which have only recently been revealed by the administrative historians like T. F. Tout, R. L. Poole, and W. H. Stevenson. This procedure was governed by the administrative structure of the country when William I conquered it, which was taken over *en bloc* as a going concern. Its main lines are now known, though there is still doubt whether the jury procedure was a Norman innovation. What Domesday Book does do is to demonstrate the way in which the Norman conception of 'feudal' tenure and the Norman idea of 'honours', each with its *caput* or centre, were reconciled after twenty years with the old structure. To spell this out in detail is the task of the historians; but

---

[1] Peter Sawyer, 'The Place-Names of the Domesday Manuscripts', *B.J.R.L.*, vol. xxxviii, No. 2, Mar. 1956.
[2] Peter Sawyer, 'The "Original Returns" and Domesday Book', *E.H.R.*, 1955.

Domesday research has advanced to the point at which it is no longer possible to doubt that the circuit *legati* from the very outset were concerned to make their returns in precisely the same form as they appear in epitome today in Volume I.

V

THE 'SATELLITE' SURVEYS

THE main sources for the history of government and administration in the Middle Ages are twofold. The activities of the central government are laid before us in the public records; while the responses which these evoked must be—somewhat painfully—reconstructed from the casually surviving but huge collections of 'custumals', like the custumal of Battle Abbey, the 'customaries', such as those of Westminster and Canterbury, and the 'cartularies' of the normal pattern produced by the obedientiaries of the many wealthy monasteries and cathedrals. Of such interaction there is no better example than the great Abbey of St. Edmunds in Suffolk. More than thirty stout volumes dating from the twelfth to the sixteenth centuries, and of the most miscellaneous character, survived the dissolution of the monasteries. Many extracts from these have appeared in print, and one of the largest, and the most miscellaneous, the vast *Pinchbeck Register*, begun by Walter Pinchbeck in 1334, has most fortunately been printed in its entirety.[1] Its contents range from charters of Cnut to the legal squabbles of the Abbey with the town at its gates; and it supplies ample evidence of the continuing importance of Domesday in the daily monastic affairs of the fourteenth century. No better example of the general process could be wished for, since the foundations of Bury stretch back to the tenth century, and by 1066 it was already a powerful franchise, with almost royal rights over the Hundreds of West Suffolk, the effects of which survive today in the division of Suffolk into the two distinct county councils of East

[1] Lord Francis Hervey, 2 vols. (1925).

and West Suffolk. Its famous Norman Abbot Baldwin, who died in 1097 or 1098, enjoyed the favour of the Conqueror, and the details of the abbey estates, preserved in Little Domesday, are known or at least knowable in greater detail than those of similar 'honours' described in Volume I. How then, we may ask, did the Domesday Survey affect the future history of the Abbey of Bury?

First, we note that the abbot's exceptional pre-Conquest powers over eight and a half Hundreds were continued and confirmed by William I, who, however, laid upon the Abbey for the first time the obligation of supplying forty armed knights for military service. This was a surprisingly heavy financial burden, since only two other abbeys, Peterborough and Glastonbury, who each owed the service of sixty knights, were more heavily burdened, and due perhaps as much to William I's support of Baldwin against the efforts of the bishop of Norwich to fix his episcopal see at Bury, as to his sheer wealth. However that may be, the problem of Bury's *servitium debitum*, as time went on and taxation changed, remained a continuing anxiety through the centuries; and the *Pinchbeck Register* 250 years later is still deeply and practically concerned with it. It preserves for us the text of Abbot John of Northwold's elaborate compilation, recording the details of the knights' fees of the Honour of St. Edmund, laboriously put together, he tells us[1] in 1300, 'from various books from the conquest of England or from the time of the enfeoffment, collected from various places, and imperfectly (*sparsim*) recorded, here brought together as I have here laboured to do'. Each knight's manors are recorded, with continual references to the Kalendar drawn up by Abbot Samson in the late twelfth century, from Domesday Book itself and from 'an old book, among the enfeoffments of Abbot Baldwin, who soon (*cito*) after the Conquest enfeoffed nearly all the knights'.[2] We are not here concerned with the details of

[1] *Pinchbeck Register*, vol. i, pp. 271 ff.   [2] Ibid., p. 273.

this process, which was set out by J. H. Round in, perhaps, the most masterly article he ever wrote.[1] But it is highly relevant to recognize that the 'knights of St. Edmund', their 'constabularies', their 'ward of Norwich Castle', and much else about them still figure largely and as a constant but slowly changing responsibility of the Abbey, not only in the *Pinchbeck Register* but in many other abbey cartularies. Indeed they provide perhaps the earliest surviving example of sub-infeudation after 1066.[2]

The monastic cartularies thus tell the story of an aristocratic multi-cellular society striving to prevent the encroachment of the central state upon their ancient privileges and their franchises. The few hundred men who, between them, owned or 'held' the whole soil of England sought from each succeeding king the confirmation of their liberties, and by the close of the Middle Ages the Charter Rolls of the royal chancery are full of long-winded charters, inspecting and confirming earlier royal charters from the time of the Norman Conquest, and, sometimes, as at Bury, still earlier. Neither sovereign nor subject could get away from the remote past. All alike were governed by custom, precedent, and century-old privilege. The struggles of Bury St. Edmunds are paralleled by all such ancient corporations, adapting Domesday Book to slowly changing administrative demands. More especially, the development of 'knights' fees' involved the rearrangement of its record and the making of continual additions. These later compilations—intensively studied in the last half-century—are the local counterpart to similar central government volumes such as the Testa de Nevill or Book of Fees. Their importance has been lately recognized in the official *Domesday Re-Bound* (1954), which refers (p. 4) to

a number of contemporary *Surveys* of the lands of certain Religious

[1] *F.E.*, pp. 225–316.
[2] The enfeoffment of Peter, *miles* of King William by Abbot Baldwin, printed by Professor D. C. Douglas (*E.H.R.*, 1927, p. 245).

Houses, the connexion of which with the Inquest of 1086 and relation to the finished *Domesday* volumes have not in some cases been clearly determined. These *Surveys* include that of Christ Church, Canterbury in the *Domesday Monachorum*; Abbot Baldwin's Feudal Book of Bury St. Edmunds; and *Surveys* made for Peterborough, Bath, Evesham, Abingdon and St. Augustine's, Canterbury.

These subsidiary documents are the key to the practical role of Domesday over the centuries. They are now often described as the 'Satellite Surveys', an unfortunate title, as Mr. Welldon Finn has pointed out, since they are for the most part not formal inquests, but monastic compilations rearranging the text of Domesday and adding thereto relevant facts of later date. They are briefly reviewed below; first because they have of recent years attracted more attention than Domesday itself; and secondly, to illustrate the immense impact of Domesday on later local history.

A. *The Feudal Book of Abbot Baldwin*[1]

The 'Liber feoffamentorum abbatis Baldewini' is called by its editor 'The Feudal Book of Baldwin'. The only surviving text is printed from a Cambridge University Library MS. of the late twelfth century, and is in three parts. The first sets out the lands of the abbot as we find them in Domesday: Hundred by Hundred and vill by vill. The second records the names and the lands of the men enfeoffed by the abbot to discharge his 'knight service'. The third, unfinished, is a list of tenants, their estates, and the money which they owe therefrom. This Feudal Book, Professor Douglas asserts, was 'the result of a survey contemporary with, but independent of, Domesday' (p. lxxvi). This conclusion rests upon his belief 'that in the initial stages of the Domesday Inquisition the greater ecclesiastical tenants-in-chief played a

[1] D. C. Douglas (ed.), *Feudal Documents from the Abbey of Bury St. Edmunds.*

prominent and an individual part. The result was, in some cases, the preparation of "private" surveys of their lands which, having been checked by independent commissioners "unknown" to their compilers, found their way with greater or less modification into the completed Domesday text.' And this belief, in turn, seems to depend upon J. H. Round's misinterpretation of the Inquisitio Comitatus Cantabrigiensis. For such wishful thinking there is no evidence; and the very language of this diligent compilation must deny its claim to be a 'Survey' of any kind. Section II, for instance, which says (in effect) this: 'Lo, here you have here the 8½ Hundreds . . . of St. Edmund . . . and this he has from the gift of the most glorious King Edward, and by concession of the most unconquerable King William, and his own son William . . . whose sealed writs bear irrefutable evidence, etc.' This is not the language of Surveys: and still less the opening of Section II: 'These are the lands of the feudal men of St. Edmund and of Baldwin the abbot which are set out above among the rest. They are therefore now written down again so that how much each man holds can be easily seen to those wishing to know it.'

What then is this 'feudal book'? It is, as Abbot John described it more than two centuries later, a book containing the enfeoffments made by Abbot Baldwin, who soon after the Conquest enfeoffed nearly all his knights. Nor is there any reason to suppose that it was compiled by Abbot Baldwin, to whose abbacy the compiler looks back with admiration, as also the reign of William II, whose sealed writs the Abbey still preserves. On the other hand, part III, at any rate, cannot be later than 1119. This was the view of R. Lennard in his *Rural England* (p. 359) who wrote:

The first two sections of the Feudal Book are based on Domesday material; but the editor's contention that the third section contains the actual 'names, estates and rents of the Domesday freemen and sokemen' is quite unacceptable, and there is really no evidence that even the first two sections were compiled by or for Abbot Baldwin, who is constantly referred to by name as one would hardly expect him to be in his lifetime.

This was the view of Abbot John of Northwold (1215–29), who carefully distinguished it from Domesday. He did not know when exactly it was made, but he realized that it had much further information; and so it had, because it belonged to a later date. On the whole we shall not be far wrong in dating it as early in the reign of Henry I, when the formal legal division was made between the Abbot's revenues and those of the Convent in the time of Abbot Robert II.[1]

B. *Domesday Monachorum of Christ Church, Canterbury*[2]
Excerpta de compoto solingorum of St. Augustine's Abbey, Canterbury[3]
Textus Roffensis from Rochester Cathedral[4]

This puzzling group of Kentish documents presents a striking contrast to Abbot Baldwin's Feudal Book from Bury St. Edmunds. In the Feudal Book we have seen one of the greatest tenants-in-chief, a great church, adapting Domesday Book, perhaps twenty years after the Survey, to its own local needs. In the Kentish documents, on the other hand, we are dealing not with Domesday Book, but with some scraps of the earlier circuit return, which was sent to Winchester and so preceded Volume I of Domesday Book. With the Kentish documents we are thus arguing backwards, from the known, which is Domesday Book, to the unknown 'circuit return' which preceded it. We are, in short, on very unsafe ground, and so thrown back constantly upon sheer hypothesis. Further

[1] Mem. of St. Edmunds Abbey 1 (Rolls Series) p. xxxvi.
[2] Ed. D. C. Douglas (R. Hist. Soc., 1944).
[3] Ed. A. Ballard, *An Eleventh Century Inquisition* (1920).
[4] Ed. T. Hearne (1720), pp. 209–11. Second copy in *Domesday Monachorum,* pp. 95–8.

research on the vast archives of Canterbury Cathedral alone may tell us more about all this in the future.

Meanwhile, several things must be borne in mind. First, then, we know that in Kent a great deal of bitter litigation had recently taken place about the lands of Canterbury which had come to a head at the Pennenden Heath trial, the very date of which is still unknown. It is even possible, though I think unlikely, that these fragments derive from an inquiry that preceded the Survey of 1086. Secondly, we must never forget that the Survey itself was made for the use of the king's household, and therefore that where we find in local archives traces of the actual proceedings of the circuit *legati*, they must have been obtained not from Winchester, but from early drafts of the circuit return, all or any of which may have been later altered before the final circuit return was sent in. This phenomenon we have already met with in Exon Domesday, and also in the Inquisitio Eliensis which was derived from an earlier draft of that circuit than the surviving Volume II of Domesday. Finally, one notes that most of the learned discussion of these documents is based on the mistaken hypothesis that the 'original returns' to Winchester were in the form of geographically compiled 'Hundred Rolls'.

With all this in mind, we may begin by considering the 'Domesday Monachorum', a term as misleading as that of 'Satellite Survey', but consecrated by time and its first student, William Somner.[1] This is a fine manuscript, in the characteristic script of Christ Church, Canterbury, superbly printed in facsimile by Professor Douglas.[2] It contains a great deal more than the descriptions of the Archbishop's lands, of the lands of his monks, and other Kentish landowners, including those of Rochester Cathedral—with which alone we are here concerned; and in particular a list of the 'knights' of the Archbishop, which

[1] *Domesday Monachorum*, p. 4. He wrote *The Antiquities of Canterbury* (1640).

[2] But still, alas, much reduced in size from that of the MS., which hides the splendour of the original.

reminds us of Abbot Baldwin's enfeoffments of the Bury
'knights'. But the 'Domesday' portion (pp. 81–98) is in
the earliest script of the manuscript and may be roughly
dated as *circa* 1100. We have thus very early copies of the
Christ Church and Rochester material.

For the lands of St. Augustine's Abbey we are dependent
on a later thirteenth-century manuscript[1] which is headed:

Excerpta de compoto solingorum comitatus cancie secundum
cartam regis videlicet ea quae ad ecclesiam sancti Augustini pertinent et est in regis Domesday.

Its value—which is considerable—is difficult to assess,
owing to the lateness of the manuscript, which has
borrowed from later material; but its description, as a
'compotus' of sullings (which correspond to 'hides' elsewhere), is consonant with a date very soon after Domesday, as we have already seen, and the Christ Church
scribes, like those at Bury, were aware that it was something different from the final record in Domesday Book.
This is demonstrable by a typical example, first, of a
place mentioned both in the Excerpta and in Domesday
Monachorum.

Excerpta	*D. Mon.*	*D.B. In Cantuarie Hund.*
In hundredo de Canterberia habet Archiepiscopus manerium Norgate et est de cibo monachorum sanctae trinitatis. Tempore regis Edwardi se defendit pro uno solino cui nunc subiacent c. burgenses xix. minus qui reddunt ix. lib. et vj. den. de gablo et est appreciatum xvij. lib. (p. 12)	Nordwda est manerium monachorum sanctae trinitatis et est de cibo eorum et est de hundred de cantuarberia et in tempore Edwardi regis se defendebat pro uno sull et ei subiacent c. burgenses iij. minus qui reddunt viij. lib. et vj. denarios de gablo et est appreciatum x. et vij. lib. Hoc manerium est de hundred de Cantuarberia. (f. 6 b)	Ipse archiepiscopus tenet Nordeude. pro uno solin se defendit. Terra est . In dominio j. caruca et dimidia. Et vij. villani cum xxvj. bordariis habent ij. carucas. Huic M pertinent in civititate canttuaria c. burgenses iij. minus reddentes viij. lib. & iiij. sol. Ibi viij. molendina de lxxj. sol. xxiiij. acrae prati. Silva xxx. porcorum. Inter totum valet et valuit xvij. lib. (D.B. I, f. 5 a l.)

---

[1] *Miscellaneous Books of the Exchequer* (K.R.), vol. 27.

Secondly we may compare a Rochester manor, of which we have a second copy in the Textus Roffensis, with the Domesday equivalent:

D. Mon.

De Falceham
  Falceham est manerium episcopi Rofensis et in tempore E. regis se defendebat pro ii sullinc et nunc similiter et est appretiatum viii libris.   (p. 69)

D.G.

Isdem episcopus tenet Fachesam. Pro ii solins se defendit. *Terra est* . *In dominio est una caruca et xv villani cum iij bordariis habent iii carucas. Ibi aecclesia et iii servi et ii molini de xv solidis et iiii acrae prati. Silva xxx porcis.* T.R.E. et post valebat viii libras.

(D.B. I, f. 5 b)

These instances show that the descriptions of the lands of Christ Church, of Rochester, and St. Augustine's in Domesday Book are based upon a common source[1] which recorded only the name of the owner, the number of 'sulungs', and the value. The leisurely formulas it employed remind us rather of Exon Domesday, as do also the different spelling of names and the use of *appreciatum* for the standard *valet* of Domesday Book. To this source have been added, in each case, the manorial details regarding demesne, villains, ploughs, etc., printed above in italics. The obvious, or at least the simplest, inference the facts suggest is that in this circuit the *legati* compiled their local return in two stages: first, the sworn oral inquest conducted in the county court which recorded only ownership, assessment, and value; secondly, the rearrangement of the geographical survey under the names of the tenants-in-chief, when it was enlarged by the inclusion of the details of the manorial economy, supplied, no doubt, 'out of court', by the actual tenants of each estate. This hypothesis is strikingly confirmed by the descriptions of the archbishop's manor of Stursete,[2]

---

[1] See *M.D.B.*, pp. 146–55, where the common source is called 'P'.
[2] Excerpta, pp. 12–13.

contained in both the Domesday Monachorum and the Excerpta. Stursete answered for seven sulungs, some of which was held in demesne and the rest by five sub-tenants, each of whose holdings is then set out apparently as a separate estate. But when we turn to Domesday Book, it is apparent that these in fact were worked as only two separate units.

This hypothesis, then, for it is no more, suggests that the descriptions of the archbishop's manors, and those of Rochester Cathedral in the Domesday Monachorum (pp. 81–98), and the Excerpta of St. Augustine's Abbey are both extracted from the common source—say P, which probably dealt with the whole of Kent and which contained further information not found in Domesday. Such a document, it might be objected, could have been made years earlier, indeed, any time after the Pennenden Heath litigation. For there is no evidence that such a clear-cut two-stage procedure was employed in any other circuit, and one feels that the restricted scope it allotted to the formal court evidence—place, owner, assessment, and value—is rather suspicious. There is, however, one vital passage common to both the Domesday Monachorum and the Excerpta which proves that P must have been a record of the Domesday Inquest, and so belongs to the year 1086. It occurs in the description of Sandwich, and runs as follows in Domesday Monachorum and Domesday Book:

D. Mon.	*D.B.*
Quando archiepiscopus recuper-avit reddebat xl. libras et xl. millia de allecibus. Et in praeter-ito anno reddidit l. libras et allecia sicut prius. Et in isto anno debet reddere lx. et x. libras et allecia sicut prius.	Quando recepit archiepiscopus reddebat xl. libras de firma et xl. milia de allecibus ad victum monachorum. *In anno quo facta est haec descriptio* reddidit Sanuuic l. libras de firma et alleces sicut prius.

The third version, in the Excerpta, varies slightly from that of Domesday Monachorum:

Et quando archiepiscopus recuperavit reddebant xl. libras et xl. milia de allecibus. Modo vero debent reddere lxx. libras et alleces sicut prius.

Though the Domesday Monachorum and the Excerpta vary from each other, they both clearly derive from the common source P. And that this troubled the *legati* is evident from the italicized words in Domesday Book. The use of this phrase in Domesday Book is excessively rare[1] and indicates some kind of ambiguity in the evidence tendered. But however we explain it, it demonstrates beyond all reasonable doubt that P, the common source, formed a part of the Survey proceedings in 1086.[2]

That the *legati* conducted their Survey in the county court is hardly to be doubted. Augustus Ballard, who printed the Excerpta, was worried regarding the order of the Kentish Hundreds in his manuscript. A close examination shows that their procedure was governed by the peculiar division of the county into five full 'lasts' or lathes, and two half-lasts, each subdivided into a number of small, shifting Hundreds. Examination shows that each 'last' formed a separate unit, perhaps a separate booklet. The difference Ballard found between the order of the Hundreds in Domesday Book and the Excerpta sprang from the inversion of the order of the two great lasts of Wyewarlest and Borowarlest.

Excerpta	*D.B.*
Sutton (half-last)	Sutton
Aylesford	Aylesford
Milton (half-last)	Milton
Wyewarlest	Borowarlest
Borowarlest	Wyewarlest
Limowarlest	Eastry
	Limowarlest

---

[1] It also occurs in D.B. I, f. 269 a 2, in Cheshire: *ipso anno hujus descriptionis.*

[2] *Domesday Monachorum*, p. 89, where all three versions are printed. Professor Douglas (p. 23) was of opinion that this entry dated D. Mon. as of the year *after* the Survey, viz. 1087. But the very form of P and its local terminology rule out this conclusion.

The last four of these are grouped in Domesday as the four lasts of East Kent whose juries agree (*concordant*) on the 'king's laws' in the country. The importance of this lies in the fact that it shows that P, the common source, antedated the final epitome now found in Volume I of Domesday.

In Kent, too, we find evidence of the difficulties encountered in discovering the intricate statistics of each estate. In scores of entries we meet with the words 'Terra est   ', the blank space showing that they had failed to discover the number of ploughs (*carucae*) which the land could sustain. And this, in turn, supports the view that for such details the clerks had to depend on evidence tendered in private between the sworn versions of the Survey, whose findings are recorded in P.

Between them, the Domesday Monachorum and the Excerpta contribute much detailed information which was included in the circuit return but omitted by its epitomizer who was responsible for Volume I of Domesday Book. It seems, for instance, to suggest that in some instances, behind the Norman sub-tenants of manors, there may have been unrecorded Saxons who continued to farm lands, the ownership of which had been transferred to Normans. But its main interest lies in the light it throws upon the precise procedure of the *legati* on this circuit. It differed markedly from both that of the south-western circuit and of East Anglia, though all three, and no doubt the rest of which we know nothing, produced returns identical in form with the shortened form in which they survived in Domesday Book.

c. '*Evesham A, a Domesday Text*', edited by
P. H. Sawyer (*Worcester Historical Society, 1960*)

This short text is printed from Cotton MS. Vespasian B xxiv, fos. 6–7ᵛ in the British Museum. The manuscript is a cartulary of Evesham Abbey, and was written about the end of the twelfth century. Though here accorded the title of 'a survey', it is, in fact, no more than a fragment, prefaced only by the words *In nomine Domini Amen* written on the upper margin of f. 6 and ending just before another fragment of which J. H. Round made good use in *Feudal England* (pp. 178 ff.). 'It has long been recognised', writes Professor Sawyer, 'that *Evesham A* is closely related to the Domesday account of Worcestershire, although the nature of the relationship has never been determined.' Round described it as an 'abstract of Domesday . . . which deserves attention as its compiler seems to have possessed some additional information'; and it is certainly true that Evesham A contains quite a lot of information not to be found in Volume I of Domesday Book. But, after a detailed analysis, Dr. Sawyer clearly demonstrates an earlier and more exciting origin. It goes right back to the actual Survey of 1086, he says, and is based on an early stage of that inquiry. It is, therefore, of importance for Domesday scholarship, and throws new light upon circuit return No. V, which included among other counties Worcestershire.

Without trying to follow Dr. Sawyer's arguments in detail, an attempt may here be made to emphasize some of its chief features. Evesham A is a list of Worcestershire estates for most of which a value is given together with an assessment in hides and virgates. 'Of the 31 tenants named, 18 are described as sub-tenants in Domesday Book, and there are good reasons for believing that the remainder were also sub-tenants at the time of the Domesday Survey, although they are not mentioned in Domesday Book.' There are also clear 'similarities of arrangement'. The accounts of Fishborough Hundred, held by Evesham Abbey, of Oswaldslaw Hundred, held by the church of Worcester, and the lands held by Pershore Abbey are all arranged in much the same order in both Evesham A and in Domesday Book. In Evesham A the estates are arranged in Hundreds, while the Worcestershire

Domesday is arranged according to the fiefs held by
tenants-in-chief. Only Ash Hundred is described in full
in the 'surviving part' of Evesham A, which attributes the
full and correct total of 100 hides against the 97½ hides in
Domesday. In the double Hundred of Pershore held by
Westminster Abbey, Domesday begins with the estates
held wholly or partly in demesne and ends with those
estates in which the Abbey had retained no demesnes. In
Evesham A the demesnes of the Abbey are also listed
first, in the same order as in Domesday Book, but the
parts of these estates which were held by sub-tenants are
here listed separately after all the demesnes have been
described.

All this and more is very complicated and even con-
fusing, for we have only a fragment of the full evidence
here described. But at least it proves that Evesham A is,
in origin, closely related to the elaborate documentation
that lay behind the evolution of the circuit return. Here
as elsewhere the Survey was concerned to make a record
of the wealth of individuals, tenants-in-chief, and their
sub-tenants. Here as elsewhere the *initial* procedure was,
as set out in the terms of reference, by the sworn testimony
in court of almost all who held lands, and the systematic
evidence of juries from each Hundred, which alone could
ensure that no estate was overlooked. Here as elsewhere
the evidence gathered geographically from the hundred
juries was on its way to becoming a record of persons.
Dr. Sawyer suggests that the ultimate source of Evesham
A may have been a compilation of information collected
from tenants-in-chief and arranged in Hundreds in
preparation for the hundredal inquiry but before that
inquiry took place. Various indications, he believes, would
be consistent with the suggestion that 'tenants-in-chief
submitted returns to the Domesday Commissioners that
were there then checked'. The difficulty about this view
lies in the fact that no clear evidence of such pre-hundredal
returns of tenants-in-chief seems to survive from any

circuit. The surviving material seems even to suggest the contrary, viz. that the first step everywhere was the sworn Inquest based on the juries of the Hundreds, and sometimes—but not in every case—put into writing. This was followed by a hectic activity between sessions of the county court, in which all kinds of people handed in the full details of each estate, and the circuit return slowly through several drafts took its final shape as we see it in Little Domesday. It is then, perhaps, asking too much of this little document that it should tell us the detailed procedure of the Inquest; but at least it takes us right back to it. It is an authentic record of 1086, and shows us, as everywhere else, the ingenious manner in which the new concept of the fief and of the tenants-in-chief was dovetailed into the old administrative structure of county and Hundred.

Dr. Sawyer is undoubtedly correct in insisting that the information in it was in some respects reorganized and altered before it became the circuit return. But the materials on which it is based may well have been more comprehensive than appear in our document. One entry, in particular—for which there is no corresponding Domesday version—is of sufficient importance to quote in full:[1]

Brichtveit habuit iii hidas una virgata minus in Walingewica[2] in tempore regis Edwardi et ita non potuit ire de domino qui Bremesgrave habuit sine licentia eius et in tempore regis Edwardi valuit xx solidos. Hanc tenet Walterus de vicecomite et cum vicecomes recepit nichil pecunie ibi recepit. Sed modo habet i carucam ii servi lxi porcos ii oves v bordarios et habent unam carucam et rex habet captum boscum et miserat in forestum et modo valet x solidos.

This entry immediately calls to mind Exon Domesday, circuit II, which uses similar leisurely formulas and meticulously records the pigs, the sheep, and the *servi*. We must not over-stretch a single entry, but is it fanciful to suggest that behind Evesham A lies a huge compilation

[1] p. 35.   [2] Willingwick (lost) in Bromsgrove.

analogous to Exon, and indicating that the local return of circuit V, though by a different procedure, produced a volume on the same generous scale? Had this survived it would have explained most of the difficulties in Evesham A, which still preserves for us much detailed information ruthlessly jettisoned in the shortened Exchequer version. However that may be, the church of Worcester must have had local access to a still unfinished draft of the local return of circuit V. This conclusion is in line with the fact that its chief additional information relates to sub-tenants,[1] the details of whose tenancies are consistently omitted in Volume I of Domesday, and clinched by its local spelling of place-names, carefully noted by Dr. Sawyer. Some characteristic instances of this process are worth quoting:

Evesham A	D.B.
Lenz Bernardi	Lenche
Croela Gualteri	Croelai
Odencote Roberti	Udecote
Cokehelle	Cochehi
Gardelegia	Gerlie

D. *Bath Abbey*

In 1893 perhaps the most rewarding, and certainly the shortest, of these peripheral Domesday documents was published by the Somerset Record Society.[2] Its impor-tance was first recognized by Baring[3] in 1912, and it was fully discussed in 1943[4] by the late Reginald Lennard, under the title of 'A Neglected Domesday Satellite', and is of particular interest to students of Exon Domesday.

---

[1] e.g. on p. 34 we are told the full story of one of the five hides at Wadberga (Wadborough). It was granted to Godric the thegn, T.R.E. for three lives, and is now held by Urse for his lifetime.

[2] William Hunt (ed.), 'Two Chartularies of the Priory of St. Peter at Bath', Somerset Record Soc., vol. vii, No. 73 (1893), pp. 67–8.

[3] 'The Exeter Domesday', *E.H.R.*, 1912, p. 309.

[4] *E.H.R.*, 1943.

Taken from a twelfth-century cartulary of the cathedral priory of St. Peter of Bath, which in 1086 was still just an ancient Benedictine abbey, it yields new and positive information upon the circuit return of the south-western counties, which is expertly set out in Lennard's article. Short as it is, the document is no fragment, but a *description* or return of the seven Somerset manors held in demesne by the Abbey in 1086.[1] The final record of these is printed in Domesday Book, Volume I, f. 89 b 2. which is a précis of the fuller Exon descriptions of pp. 171–3. The Bath document has close affinities with the Exon version, but contains substantial additional information, and so is shown to be independent of it. Herein lies the importance of the Bath version, as can be seen by printing the three surviving accounts of the manor of Lyncombe.

D.B. I, f. 89 b 2

Ipsa aecclesia tenet LINCOME. T.R.E. geldabat pro x hidis. Terra est viii carucis. De ea sunt in dominio vii hidae et ibi iii carucae et viii servi et iiii villani et x bordarii cum iii carucis. Ibi ii molini reddant x solidos et xxx acrae prati et cc acrae pasturae. Valuit vi libras. Modo viii libras.

Exon Domesday, p. 172

Abbas habet i mansionem quae vocatur Lincuma quam tenuit Seuuoldus abbas tempore Eduuardi regis et reddit gildum pro x hidis has possunt viii carrucas. Inde habet Abbas vii hidas et iii carrucas in dominio et villani ii hidas et iii carrucas. Ibi habet Abbas iiii villanos et x bordarios et viii servos et i runcinum et viii porcos et clxxx oves et ii molendina qui reddunt per annum x solidos et xxx agros prati et cc agros pascue. Haec modo valet per annum viii libras et quando abbas recepit valebat vi libras.

Bath Cartulary

Abbas Bathoniensis habet i mansionem quae vocatur Lincoma. Haec se defendebat tempore regis Edwardi pro x hidis. *De his*

---

[1] The argument turns on the grant of Charlecombe to William Hosatus ('Two Chartularies', no. 33, pp. 37–8)—a document which mentions William Hosatus as still living.

habuit quidam tagnus Osuuardus iiii hidas et dimidiam tempore Regis Edwardi. Et hic tagnus non poterat auferre terram suam de abbatia. Hic sua spontanea voluntate remisit terram suam in abbatiam, licet has iiii hidas et dimidiam quas superius dixi.[1] *De his habet modo Walterus Hosatus i hidam de abbate, et alterae sunt in abbatia.* De his x hidis praedictis habet abbas in dominio vii, et homines sui habent iii hidas. Has omnes insimul possunt arare vii carrucae. Ibi habet abbas in dominio iii carrucas, et homines iiii. Ibi habet abbas iiii villanos, et x cocetos, et viii servos, et i runcinum, et ii molendinos qui reddunt x solidos per annum, et viii porcos, et cc oves xx minus, et xxx agros prati, et cc agros pascuae. Et quando abbas recepit hanc mansionem valebat vi libras, et modo valet viii.

The Bath cartulary's account of Priston similarly contains three statements not found in either Exon or Volume I of Domesday:

1. *Et haec* [sc. *mansio*] *fuit de victu monachorum tempore regis Edwardi.*
2. *Ex his* [sc. *vi hidis*] *geldaverunt iiii hidae ea die qua rex Edwardus fuit vivus et mortuus.*
3. *Et homines franci habent ibi xxv animalia et xii oves.*

The words in italics are thus peculiar to the Bath descriptions of these demesne manors. On the other hand, Exon Domesday contains facts not found in the Bath document, as Lennard explained:

> Of five manors it says that Abbot Sewold (who seems to have been joint-abbot with Wulfwold) held the manor on the day King Edward was alive and dead (or in King Edward's time), and of the remaining two that the Abbot (*ipse*) held them at that time. And for the last three manors in the Bath list the Exon Domesday gives values, and for the last two manors live-stock figures also which are wanting (for these manors) in the Bath text.

With the patient ingenuity of which he was a master, Lennard next discusses the varying order of the Hundreds in the three documents, and their different phraseology.

---

[1] The use of the first person suggests—as Lennard points out—that the scribe is adding to his original from local knowledge.

In every case Bath has *se defendebat*, while Exon says *reddit gildum*; and Exon uses *nemusculum* (altered in Domesday to *silva minuta*) for land described in the Bath text as *pascua*; and finally he records differences in the valuations and the spelling of names.

His final verdict is stated thus:

> On the whole it seems to me probable that the Bath text was not derived from the Exon text but belongs to a still earlier stage of the Domesday Inquest . . . It may be that that text is, or is based upon, a return of demesne manors made by the Abbey itself; that this return was submitted to the Commissioners: and that they then checked and supplemented the information contained in it in the light of the jurors' verdicts.

There is much more of interest in Lennard's analysis. Although he wrote before it was known that the geld accounts in Exon belonged, not to 1084, but to 1086, he correctly identified the Bath document as a *complete* return of the Abbey's manors then held in demesne, despite the apparent omission of 'Eveslie' and Ashwick. He has also much of interest to say about a second text in the cartulary, headed 'De terris Bathae pertinentibus'. But the supreme value of his article lies in the warning it contains against over-simplification of the complicated procedure of the Inquest of 1086, and the danger of drawing over-hasty conclusions. Altogether it is a model of acute Domesday scholarship.

E. *Peterborough* (*Society of Antiquaries MS. 60*)

This manuscript, called the 'Liber Niger',[1] is a twelfth-century cartulary of the Abbey of Peterborough, which still awaits scholarly diplomatic analysis, though much used by Domesday students. It contains at least two separate documents of great importance for Domesday inquiry.

---

[1] See G. R. C. Davis, *Medieval Cartularies of Great Britain* (1958), nos. 754 and 763 for an account of this MS. Cf. Dugdale, *Monasticon*, i, p. 372.

I. The first, written in English, records the collection of a geld in Northamptonshire, the precise date of which is uncertain, but probably falls between 1072 and 1078.[1] First printed by Ellis in his *Introduction to Domesday* (1833), vol. i, pp. 184–7, it has been lately reissued in Miss A. J. Robertson's *Anglo-Saxon Charters* (1939), pp. 231–6. Perhaps the most important fact about it is that it is written in English, of which the editor supplies a modernized version. Its importance was first noted by J. H. Round in one of his most brilliant articles in *Feudal England* (pp. 147–56).

II. A second important document from the 'Liber Niger' was printed as an Appendix to Thomas Stapleton's *Chronicon Petroburgense* (Camden Soc., 1849), pp. 157 –83. It falls into three distinct parts: first, a minute, manorial description of the abbey lands, pp. 157–68; next, a list of the knights of Peterborough, pp. 168–76, on which Round commented in *Feudal England*, pp. 157– 65; and thirdly, the Lindsey Survey, pp. 176–83, which was reproduced in facsimile, with a translation by James Greenstreet (London, 1884).[2] On this 'invaluable' Survey Round also wrote at length in *Feudal England*, pp. 181– 95.

Each of these documents calls for some brief comment.

1. *The Northamptonshire Geld Roll*

The title is something of a misnomer, which, however, it would be now pedantic to alter. A single Hundred will suffice to show the form of the document; and it is taken from Miss Robertson's modernized version (p. 233):

To Egelweardesle Hundred belong 100 hides, as was the case in King Edward's time, and of these, 16 hides and half a hide have paid geld and 40 hides are in demesne, and from $6\frac{1}{2}$ hides at Norton not a penny has been received—Osmund, the King's secretary (*writere*) owns that estate—and 37 hides are waste.

---

[1] Stenton, *Anglo-Saxon England*, p. 636 n. 3.
[2] Cf. Gross, *Sources . . . of English History* (1915), no. 1904.

Osmund appears to have been the king's Chancellor, and, if so, the list is before 1078, when he became bishop of Salisbury. Each Hundred begins thus, with a statement of the number of hides it contains, followed by the number which have actually paid the geld, at whatever rate per hide it was charged. Next follows demesne or 'in land', which was exempt from tax, and then the six and a half hides at Norton, already exempt from tax as long afterwards in the Pipe Rolls, because they belonged to an officer of the king's household. Last of all comes the land exempted as 'waste', the 'almost incredible amount of which'—to quote Round—bears out the English chronicler's account of the 'ravages' in the autumn of 1065.

> The Northerners did much damage around Northampton: not only did they slay men and burn houses and corn, but carried off all the livestock they could find, amounting to many thousands. They took many hundreds of captives, and carried them off north with them, so that the shire and the other neighbouring shires were for many years the poorer.[1]

The supreme importance of this county list lies in the fact that it is still an English document at a time when Latin had supplanted English as the language of government records. Here we see, as Stenton pointed out, 'the type of record' current in England before 1066; and in this connection one notes that the assessment of every Hundred has remained the same since 'the time of King Edward'.

On no point of Domesday criticism have the experts gone further astray than in this matter of the geld. It was confused in the Victorian mind with the notion of 'direct parliamentary taxation', abandoned in 1051, and thought to have been only very occasionally levied after the Conquest. From such thinking arose the universally held opinion that the Conqueror's aim in 1086 was to ascertain

---

[1] *Anglo-Saxon Chronicle*, tr. Garmonsway, p. 192. The statistics of the whole twenty-eight Hundreds are succinctly tabulated by Round, *F.E.*, p. 153.

from the Survey, *all* the facts with a view to reassessing geld on a more just basis. We have seen above that such a view is incorrect[1], and the Northampton list—a lone survivor—must now be thought of as typical of thousands of just such documents—earlier and later—recording levies of this ancient custom, collected at the king's pleasure, ever more often as the reign of William I continued. The money was collected, Hundred by Hundred, according to the immemorial assessment attributed to 'the time of King Edward'. By the close of the reign, its collection had become virtually annual.

With this firmly in our minds, we may turn to the *Inquisitio geldi* in Exon Domesday, for the five south-western counties. This was a separate sworn inquest, immediately preceding the Survey of 1086, of which we have not got the original text, but only varying accounts of the actual sums collected, which differ from one another and are still incomplete. From these we learn that the *inquisitio geldi* on which they are based had brought to light many geldable hides which had lain concealed ever since the 'custom' was relieved from the moment of the Conquest. And a comparison of these accounts with the text of Exon Domesday shows that the Domesday *legati* took account of these long 'lost hides'. That a similar 'geld inquest' was carried out and used by the 1086 *legati* in other circuits is no more than an assumption, though a reasonable one,[2] in view of Robert of Hereford's testimony regarding the excitement caused in 1086 'by the collection of the royal money'. But, at least, the collectors' accounts in the south-west of the geld taken apparently in 1085–6 destroy the hypothesis of a benevolent king revising a

[1] p. xv.

[2] The survival of these tax accounts in Exon was probably due to an oversight on the part of the *legati* on this circuit. As elsewhere, they collected their evidence from the juries of the Hundreds in each county, which they regrouped according to the fees of each tenant-in-chief, but without specifying in what Hundred each constituent manor lay. The tax accounts, being arranged by Hundreds, no doubt assisted the compilation of the circuit return to Winchester, the abbreviated version of which survives in Vol. I of Domesday Book.

system of direct taxation on humanitarian lines. Actually, it was a hasty preliminary, whose records were used to enforce payment from 'lost hides', which were duly noted in the actual Survey of 1086. The Crown was concerned only to extract every penny due to it.

Maitland's conclusion that the 'one main object'[1] of the king's commissioners in 1086 was the 'quest for geld' is false. But this should not be taken to imply that geld was not a major preoccupation of the circuit *legati*. Contrariwise, geld was so important as to produce a *preliminary* inquest to correct the ancient assessment in use since 'King Edward's day'; and the results of this inquest were embodied in the Domesday Survey. The purposes of the Survey, however, were far wider and more fundamental—no less than an actuarial assessment of the national wealth arranged according to the new feudal order. In this operation the geld was of higher importance than even Round and Maitland knew, for by 1086 it had become a virtually annual levy, and so remained for another century. Throughout this period and even longer, the geld assessment of every manor was a matter of practical importance to the king's sheriffs and bailiffs. But far more important was the detailed record of the value of the Crown lands and those of the tenants-in-chief. The main financial objects of the Survey only became known to us from the later Pipe Rolls, which record, county by county, the huge increase of revenue made possible by the Survey—the county 'farms'; the fines, oblations, the escheats, wardships, etc.—all of which were now accurately measurable in terms of pounds, shillings, and pence.

11. *The Appendix to the* Chronicon Petroburgense (*Camden Soc., 1849, pp. 157–83*)

Stapleton's Appendix to the Chronicon Petroburgense (ff. 6–74) is a survey of the Abbey's manors compiled by the central government between 1125 and 1128. It is

---

[1] *D.B.B.*, p. 5.

written in a twelfth-century book hand with rubrics and plain red initials, and must be carefully distinguished from the rest of its various contents. It is one of the earliest, and certainly the most important, 'survey' drawn up after that of 1086, and serves as a bridge uniting Domesday with the innumerable monastic compilations of later centuries. It is also a true 'survey'[1] drawn up by the central government, though just how we have no information. Its contents have been minutely compared with the Domesday (1086) account of Peterborough by Stenton in his 'Types of Manorial Structure in the Northern Danelaw', following in the footsteps of Round's articles in *Feudal England*. The men who made it 'were conversant with the formulas of the Exchequer, who had derived, from whatever source, information respecting the ownership of certain of the monastic estates at a period as remote as the time of King Edward'.[2] But its chief interest lies in the fact that this Survey sets out the facts, not from the point of view of a local abbey reporting its holdings to the central government, but from that of the tenant-in-chief enjoying their revenues, who by the accident of a vacancy is the king himself.

The first section (pp. 157–66) contains manorial descriptions of the abbey manors, spread over several counties, with a wealth of detail nowhere found in Domesday Book. It is in fact one of the earliest 'custumals' setting out the holdings and labour services of the whole peasantry, and distinguishing carefully the land held by sokemen, by 'bordars', the land held by military service, and the land held by 'pleni villani' and 'semi-villani',[3] and

---

[1] David Knowles, *The Monastic Order in England* (1940), p. 613 n. 6, quotes the Peterborough historian Hugh Candidus (1124): 'Rex misit justiciarios suos Ricardum Basset et Walterum archidiaconum et . . . descripserunt omnes thesauros ecclesiae et omnem abbatiam, et quicquid erat intus et foris, et attulerunt ad regem, rex tenuit abbatiam in manu sua.'

[2] F. M. Stenton, 'Types of Manorial Structure in the Northern Danelaw', *Oxford Studies in Social and Legal History*, vol. ii (1910), p. 6.

[3] Cf. Vinogradoff, *English Society in the Eleventh Century*, p. 448.

giving a detailed summary of the stock on each manor, the hides 'ad geldum regis', and the 'value'. We also read of 'pleni cotseti'. This section closes (pp. 166–8) with a summary of the 'redditus maneriorum de Burch'; it also states that in the Abbey were sixty monks, and gives details of their infirmary, kitchen, and much else.

The second section (pp. 168–76) contains the list of the knights of Peterborough already enfeoffed by the abbot; and the third what is known as the Lindsey Survey, which seems to derive from documents of the very beginning of the twelfth century.[1] The terminology of these Peterborough documents and the similar extents in the Burton cartulary[2] is in general reconcilable with that of Domesday Book, and while they form a link with the many late extents, they also provide continuity for research, like that of Vinogradoff and Maitland on pre-Conquest economic arrangements.

Two conclusions are suggested by the above review of some of the so-called 'Domesday Satellites'. The first is, beyond all question, the dominating and continuing importance of the Survey of 1086 for several centuries after it was compiled. It blazed a trail, for there is nothing remotely comparable with it of earlier date either in England or abroad. It was indeed, as it was meant to be, a record of the new feudal order, in which the ownership of all land was divided between the Crown—with its ancient demesne—and the fiefs of some hundreds of tenants-in-chief, who together formed medieval society for centuries to come. As late as 1215, the fourteenth clause of Magna Carta laid down that the royal council should consist of the greater barons, summoned individually by writ, and in addition 'all those who hold of us in chief', summoned generally by the king's sheriffs and bailiffs. It was, of

---

[1] Stenton, 1884, op. cit., p. 7.
[2] Ed. Wrottesley (Salt Society, 1884); and see Round, 'The Burton Abbey Surveys' *E.H.R.*, 1935, pp. 275–89.

course, no more than a 'paper constitution', practically impossible, but at least it retained the theory of society envisaged by Domesday Book. So long as earldoms, baronies, knights' fees, aids, and scutages survived, Domesday Book retained its utility. Many other important government compilations dealt with the ever-developing institutions: books like the Red Book of the Exchequer, the Book of Fees, and innumerable later Surveys. But the whole set-up went back to Domesday Book, without which the development, and sometimes the very identification, of royal demesne would have been in doubt, and the vital part played by genealogy impossible. Its influence is continuously traceable from reign to reign, and the two volumes of Domesday were continually transported from London, when the central administration was removed from the capital; and its evidence is still accepted in the law courts. It remains to sketch below the persistent force of this pattern document at least until the late fourteenth century.

The second conclusion suggested by this review is the rapidity with which the manorial descriptions in Domesday went out of date, so that almost from the day it was completed, it demanded radical alteration. This is perfectly illustrated by the Liber Niger of Peterborough discussed above, and explains better than anything else why the local returns of the circuits were drastically 'cut' in the two surviving original volumes. Within years of its completion, the landlord, be he king or tenant-in-chief, required to get the extraordinarily detailed rents and services on every manor restated in order to exploit his property. So while in the twelfth century 'custumals' multiplied and replaced the Domesday summaries, the more permanent elements of the Survey of 1086 were preserved in the abbreviations of Domesday Book treated below. The main structure of the Survey remained essential—the county lists of royal demesne, and of the fees of tenants-in-chief: the geldable 'hides' on each manor, and the 1086 'owners' or tenants—for these set out the abiding facts of tenure and barony discovered by the Survey. All else was omitted from the abbreviated version, of which enough copies remain to suggest that far more have perished, and much research remains to be done on these 'breviates'. They are, after all, the best evidence for the abiding importance of the *descriptio* of 1086 in both local and central government.

VI

AFTER DOMESDAY: HEREFORDSHIRE DOMESDAY AND THE BREVIATE

EVER since F. W. Maitland wrote *Domesday Book and Beyond* (1897) historians have recognized its importance for Anglo-Saxon history. But in this new awareness of its backward-looking importance, they are now in danger of overlooking its still greater—indeed dominating—influence upon later medieval history. Mr. Richardson and Mr. Sayles, two seasoned experts in a work full of new thinking, have carried this reaction to a point bordering on absurdity. They speak of Domesday as a 'vast administrative mistake', the result of a 'personal whim of William I, a man of very limited vision, narrow, ignorant and superstitious', and deplore 'the inability of its unknown planner to concentrate his attention upon a practical objective', and so conclude[1] 'Within a generation Domesday Book itself had become a historical monument, respected but unused.' To me, this too eloquent judgement is more than an exaggeration: it approaches the reverse of the truth. The unknown planner of Domesday Book–if indeed he *is* unknown— set out to produce a 'blue print' of a new society, so simple and so handy as to serve as a practical guide to the king's Treasury officials for an indefinite future. The making of Domesday Book was not the conclusion, but the beginning of its history.

The failure of recent historians to appreciate the living persistence of Domesday Book through later centuries springs from the neglect of administrative history; and it is heightened by the modern habit of writing medieval

[1] *The Governance of Medieval England* (Edinburgh, 1963), p. 28.

history in 'periods', whereby each author makes a new beginning and strives, at all costs, to avoid repetition. It may even owe something to the effort, conscious or unconscious, 'to get away from Stubbs', who described Domesday as 'an exhaustive register of the land and its capabilities . . . *which was never entirely superseded*'. Whatever the reasons, the revolutionary and abiding results of what Professor Le Patourel has lately described as 'the Norman colonisation of Britain' are underrated and so misunderstood in much recent work. This Norman colonization was a long process during which men from Northern France made huge landed fortunes in England. They, or the greater among them, formed a small aristocratic group, closely knit by family and feudal relationships, and in many cases claimed kinship with William himself. These men did a great deal of the conquering and taking possession of England, and their acquisitiveness was as important as the military ability of the Conqueror: 'About one fifth of the land of Domesday England was retained by the king and his immediate family: about a quarter more was held by no more than eleven great barons. There were only about 80 estates in all worth more than £100 a year.'[1] For two centuries at least, the real stuff of English history lies in the descent of these earldoms, baronies, honours, and knights' fees which have engaged the labours successively of William Farrer and Sir Charles Clay. Thanks to the Conquest, England became a satellite of France, and the most 'feudal' of all states, as the king's aristocratic entourage throughout this long period never scrupled to remind him. The day-to-day activities of the king's household bureaucracy were ceaselessly devoted to what we should now call family brawls, and that the king's sheriffs were similarly engaged is recorded in the 31 Henry I Pipe Roll. During the anarchy of Stephen's

[1] John Le Patourel, *The Norman Colonisation of Britian*, (Spoleto, 1969), p. 420.

reign, there are no Pipe Rolls, but they take up, in identical form, with Henry II's accession. Any wonder then that the old Treasurer, Richard Fitz Nigel, in his 'Dialogue concerning the Exchequer' (c. 1176) expatiates on Domesday Book:

> Domesday Book about which you inquire, is the inseparable companion in the Treasury of the royal seal . . . This book is metaphorically called by the native English, Domesday, i.e. the Day of Judgment. For as the sentence of that strict and terrible last account cannot be evaded by any skilful subterfuge, so when this book is appealed to . . . its sentence cannot be quashed or set aside with impunity.[1]

Domesday Book, he further tells us, was the finishing touch of William's effort to supersede the 'Mercian Law', the Danelaw, and the Wessex Law—all customary and unwritten—by bringing the people under a written code (*iure scripto*), or as we should say 'getting the facts down on paper'. And his whole book is, broadly speaking, a commentary upon the Pipe Rolls.

Richard Fitz Nigel's book is a solid, civil service, testimony to the enduring usefulness of Domesday, which is backed up by other casual memoranda like that of a clerk on a plea roll of 1221:

> Remember to look up Domesday Book for the bishop[2]

whose research is perhaps summarized by this letter:

> To my very dear lord Robert prior of Bath, William of Palermo, greeting. I have found in Domesday Book that the town of Bath with Easton used to geld with the shire of Somerset for 20 hides. There are also in the said town forty messuages which pay four pounds a year. There are also seven empty houses and a house which a certain interpreter holds for two shillings. The barons of the province also have in the same town fifty shillings. Farewell.[3]

[1] *Dialogus de Scaccario*, ed. Charles Johnson (1950), p. 62.
[2] *Curia Regis Rolls*, 5–6 Henry III, (1949), p. 68.
[3] Henry Ellis, *Original Letters*, 3rd Series, i. 26.

This again is a practical business matter, unless we ante-date by many centuries antiquarian interest in Domesday. So much may serve to show that the preservation of Domesday Book is 'no lucky survival' which serves as 'a boon to a learned posterity'; and the suggestion carried by these passages is very fully substantiated by the official fortunes of the Survey, through the twelfth and thirteenth centuries.

William the Conqueror died on 9 September 1087, and was buried at Caen, having commended to Arch-bishop Lanfranc his second son William as the right man to succeed him. William hurried to England; seized the Treasury at Winchester and was crowned by Lanfranc at Westminster on 26 September. During these three weeks England had no king and no official government, and the only information we have regarding the new household of William II is that he retained Gerard, later bishop of Hereford (1096–1101) as chancellor and keeper of his seal. Of the Treasury officials we know nothing. Our only hard evidence comes from surviving royal writs. The earliest of these is an original relating to Westminster Abbey which is of undoubted authenticity although it is strangely dated as *post descriptionem totius Anglie*,[1] which implies that the Survey was completed before the king's death.[2] A later writ[3] of Rufus refers to lands of St. Benet Hulme recorded (*inbreviata*) in 'my records (*meis brevibus*) in my Treasury at Winchester', which are duly mentioned in Little Domesday. There are other similar references, suggesting that they were initiated by officials familiar with the Survey. In all these the term *breve* is used in the same manner, that is as the recorded list of individual

---

[1] *Facsimiles of English Royal Writs*, ed. T. A. M. Bishop and P. Chaplais (1957), pl. XXIV.

[2] See *Anglo-Saxon England*, p. 647 n., where Stenton writes 'there is an over-whelming probability that the volumes were written . . . before the confiscations after the revolt of 1088', thus confirming the evidence of this writ.

[3] *Regesta*, vol. i, Appendix LXXX.

'honours': the King had his *breve*, and so too, each tenant-in-chief. Finally a royal writ of uncertain date[1] refers to Hayling Island which Queen Emma gave to the cathedral priory of Winchester 'as the King's book testifies' (*sicut liber regius hoc testatur*). The writ is attested by the bishop of Durham, but whether the William who took part in the Survey, or Ranulf Flambard who succeeded him in 1099 we do not know. This is the earliest reference to the Survey as a book. A later writ[2] of Queen Matilda issued between 1108 and 1113 describes a *plea* held before her in which Faritius, abbot of Abingdon, in the king's court at Winchester in the Treasury (*in thesauro*) proved his claim to Lewknor *per librum de thesauro*. Thus, as the men who had made the Survey died off, younger royal officials fumbled for a way of referring to Domesday Book; and within half a century the problem was settled by adopting the popular description of it simply as Domesday.

The possibility that the notorious Ranulf Flambard was concerned with the first known reference to the Survey as Domesday Book is of very special interest. The Norman chronicler Orderic Vitalis has a rather muddled story of Ranulf revising the Domesday Survey 'by the rod', which is borne out by a writ of Rufus[3] telling his justices to assess (*admensuretis*) the Abbey of Thorney 'for gelds, scots, knight service and all customs . . . as leniently as any honour which has the same amount of land'. Ranulf was a royal chaplain, at the centre of things at a time of great administrative advance, and Orderic's story suggests that the Survey was engaging officials all through the reign; and he was rewarded with a bishopric

---

1 'Royal Charters to Winchester', *E.H.R.*, 1920, p. 389.

2 *Abingdon Chronicle* (Rolls Series), vol. II, p. 116.

3 See *M.D.B.*, p. 211. There is a similar writ of Henry I regarding the Abbey of Ramsey, *Regesta*, vol. ii, no. 650. See R. W. Southern, 'Ranulf Flambard and Early Anglo-Norman Administration', *Trans. R. Hist. Soc.*, 1933; also pp. 183–205 in his *Medieval Humanism* (1970). 'Flambard', says Dr. Southern, 'initiated the tireless search for money for foreign conquest which is the hall-mark of English government in the Middle Ages' (p. 188).

in 1099. Three years earlier Samson, another royal chaplain, who had had much to do with the Survey of 1086, and more particularly with the compilation[1] of Great Domesday, had been made bishop of Worcester, at the same time as Gerard was given the bishopric of Hereford. Gerard and Samson, both inherited from his father by Rufus, must have done him yeoman service, for no Norman king was slower than Rufus in making new bishops.

Our evidence, not plentiful, thus suggests that to the officials who had been in royal service under William I, Domesday was regarded as a statement of national wealth, arranged under the names of tenants-in-chief, each of whom had his 'breve' or schedule in those counties wherein he held land. The newer men, like Flambard, saw it as the 'book' it was, albeit in two volumes, and within a generation it was popularly so described. But all this rests upon no more than two references to the Survey as a book, the second of which may only reflect the attitude of Queen Matilda's chancery. They are important as our most solid proof that Great Domesday (Vol. I) was strictly contemporary, that it was already *there* in the reign of Rufus. Not that there is any real ground for doubt, thanks to our three 'originals' of the Survey. But Henry I's reign, taken as a whole, uses a new terminology and this is reflected in our local evidence, notably that of Heming's Cartulary. The normal practice of this reign is to refer to Domesday —and it was in great demand—as *carta mea Wintonie*, or *compotus hidarum cartae regis*, or *carta* (or *cartula*) *regis de thesauro*. An eleventh-century Inquisition of St. Augustine's Canterbury published by Ballard[2] is headed: 'Excerpta de compoto solingorum comitatus Cancie secundum cartam regis viz. ea que ad ecclesiam Sancti Augustini pertinent, et est in registro Domesday.' The last five words may well be due to the later copyist, but a

---

[1] Above, p. 50.
[2] *Records of Social and Economic History*, vol. iv (British Academy, 1920). See also above, p. 78 n. 3.

wealth of evidence makes it clear that within a generation of its compilation, Domesday, now much out of date, was thought of as, above all, a book of Hides, or Hidage, invaluable for settling the incidence of geld. It had constantly to be buttressed by new inquiries like those of Worcester, Leicester, Lindsey, and Northampton, which were examined by J. H. Round in his *Feudal England*. But it was also invaluable as a guide, however imperfect, to the great honours and baronies created by William I, and to the details of 'royal demesne'.

This slowly changing view of Domesday is reflected by two large experiments which have been virtually ignored by historians. Together they provide indisputable evidence of the enduring practical employment of the Survey by the central government, by the sheriffs of counties, and by the great landowners.

I. We may begin with the splendid transcript of Herefordshire Domesday, written *c.* 1160–70, in the most formal or set hand of the royal scriptorium, used by the scribes of the itinerant Chancery and the stationary Exchequer. It is preserved for us in Balliol College MS. No. 350 and has been reproduced in facsimile by the Pipe Roll Society.[1] The script alone is proof that the manuscript emanated from the royal curia, and its illuminated initials and bold marginal rubrics show that no expense was spared by the compiler, that in fact it was made *de luxe* in the first half of Henry II's reign, when the young king's officials were striving to repair, if hardly the collapse, at least the disorder of the king's finances during the nineteen unhappy years of Stephen's reign. Why, then, was it made? The answer is furnished by the marginal rubrics, which, for easy reference, boldly repeat in red the name of each manor, and the number of 'hides' there. This suggests that it was in daily official use, a conclusion confirmed by the fact that for approximately a third of the

[1] *Herefordshire Domesday*, ed. V. H. Galbraith and J. Tait (Pipe Roll Soc., 1950).

Herefordshire manors, various scribes strove to bring it up to date by entering the names of the contemporary holders. The king's officials were financially interested in the descent of fiefs and manors; and the marginal entry for each of its hide assessments, as well as some valuable *addenda*, indicate that the shire officials were still concerned about the collection of geld. And close examination shows that the names of 'present' holders of manors were being added piecemeal for some twenty or thirty years after it was written. But though a completely official product of the royal scriptorium, it strikes us as also a personal experiment, set on foot by a very great man. Who then had it copied? To this question the answer—all but certain—is Thomas Brown, *Thomas cognomento Brunus*, the greatest 'free lance' ever let loose on English official finance. 'The Dialogue concerning the Exchequer'[1] tells the whole story:

Then, at the head of the fourth bench, opposite the justices, sits Master Thomas Brown. He is no inconsiderable person at the Exchequer. For it is a great and strong proof of his loyalty and prudence that so wise a prince chose him to have a third roll not contemplated by the ancient constitution of the Exchequer, in which to set down the laws of the realm and the royal finances, to keep it in his own hands and to carry it about with him whithersoever he will. He also has a clerk in the Lower Exchequer, who sits next the Treasurer's Clerk, and has full freedom to take notes of all receipts and expenses of the Treasury . . .

He was a great man at the court of the great King of Sicily [Roger II], a prudent counsellor and almost at the head of the King's finances (*regiis secretis*). But there arose a new King who 'knew not Joseph', one who kept bad company and persecuted his father in the persons of his servants. So Thomas fell from power and had to flee for his life.

There were many kingdoms where he would have been received with honour. But as he had been frequently invited by our noble King Henry, he preferred . . . to return to his native land and his hereditary liege lord. The King received him as befitted them

---

[1] *Dialogus de Scaccario*, ed. C. Johnson, p. 35.

both ... He has his seat at the Exchequer ... and takes part with the
magnates in all the great affairs of the Exchequer.

Thomas Brown came to England in 1158, and held his
extraordinary post until his death in 1180. Throughout
this period he received 5*d.* a day from the farm of Herefordshire, and built four houses there. The attribution of
Herefordshire Domesday to him is clinched by the
inclusion in it of a statement of the king's religious
oblations on the great feast days of the year; for Thomas
Brown held the household post of king's almoner for at
least ten years. Thus the Balliol MS. and the Dialogus
both bear witness to the practical value of Domesday
Book in royal administration nearly a century after its
compilation. As taxation concentrated more and more on
'the knights' fee', at least two other great compilations
were made by the administration, which guided royal
finance for long periods. These were the Book of Fees,
long known as the 'Testa de Nevill', and the Red Book of
the Exchequer. Medieval taxation relied overwhelmingly
on precedent, but from time to time the Exchequer would
make a new inquiry, which would serve until it too went
out of date and was itself superseded. In this backward-
looking manner, medieval finance lumbered on through
the Middle Ages, controlled by its past. But both the
Book of Fees and the Red Book were held to be just
'good evidence' of earlier procedure, while Domesday
Book was intended to be, and was from the beginning,
'final' in its findings or, as the Middle Ages expressed it,
'of record'.

Herefordshire Domesday, though written in the
Exchequer, is not a public record and comes to us from
Herefordshire. This anomaly is explained by the unique
position held by Master Thomas Brown; and its provenance, together with the documents added to it, connect
its use more with the county and the sheriff than headquarters. It is clearly related to the annual county records

in the Pipe Rolls, and it serves to show how important to the local officials in Henry II's reign Domesday still was.

II. A second splendid Domesday manuscript,[1] of Exchequer provenance, survives in the Public Record Office. This is the so-called 'Breviate' or abbreviated version of the original, written about the second quarter of the thirteenth century, perhaps by Alexander Swereford. It is handsomely illuminated, and its unrubbed, mint condition suggests that it was made for ornament rather than for use. Two later thirteenth-century copies of this book, which once belonged—strangely—to the abbeys of Margam and Strata Florida in Wales, also survive, the former as Arundel MS. 153, in the British Museum, and the other as K. R. Miscellaneous Books, No. 1, in the Public Record Office. All three are something of a mystery. There is ample evidence from both the thirteenth and fourteenth centuries of the original Domesday Book being transported on those occasions when the Exchequer was moved from London, and also of departmental writs ordering an official search to be made on various matters, especially regarding the royal demesne. Why, then, one wonders, was this costly, *de luxe* abbreviation made at so late a date?

To this question the answer seems to be that it was a fair copy of an earlier one which had been extensively used both centrally and locally in the twelfth century. The evidence for this view is limited, but definite, for we also have in MS. Vitellius C. 8 in the British Museum an abbreviated twelfth-century Domesday of Kent. But still earlier use of a radically abbreviated Domesday is found in the earliest surviving Worcester cartulary compiled by Heming, a Worcester monk at the very end of the eleventh century, and almost certainly before the year 1118.[2] Heming says he undertook his compilation at the instigation of the saintly Bishop Wulfstan, and its special interest

---

[1] Miscellaneous Books (T.R.), No. 284.
[2] *Hemingi Chartularium*, ed. Thomas Hearne, 1723.

for us lies in the fact that Wulfstan's successor as bishop
was Samson, the chaplain (1096–1112), who there is
other evidence to suppose may have been 'the man behind
Domesday Book'.[1] First, one notes that Heming supplies
(p. 287) a copy of the famous entry in Domesday, Volume
I (f. 172 b 1) regarding the church of Worcester's special
rights in the triple Hundred of Oswaldslaw—which he
slightly 'improves', and to which he adds the names of the
legati of this circuit. The passage ends thus: 'Ad huius
rei confirmationem exemplar eius in autentica regis cartula
. . . scriptum est que in thesaura regali cum totius Anglie
descriptionibus conservatur' (f. 132ᵛ).[2] Later (f. 135ᵛ) he
sets out a description of the Worcester manors with the
heading 'Descriptio terre episcopatus Wigornensis ec-
clesie, secundum cartam regis que est in thesaura regali'.
Then follows a highly abbreviated version of Domesday,
Volume I, which is, if not verbally, yet substantially
identical with that of the thirteenth-century Breviate in
the Public Record Office. Further examination might well
prove that the official Breviate text was already in existence at the beginning of the twelfth century and was the
source of Heming's version. If so, he did not hesitate to
amend his original. Of greater importance is the discovery
that within twenty years of the Survey, landlords were
already recording and using its permanent and lasting
data, while discarding the more ephemeral particulars.
No one is likely to have realized this sooner than Bishop
Samson of Worcester when Heming wrote. And the copy
de luxe of the Breviate made more than a century later
seems to testify to its popularity during the interval. It is
also of great interest to find a writer fully acquainted with
the details of the Survey (*descriptio*) of 1086, referring to
the official return in royal custody as the king's *carta* or
cartula, a term then also current in the king's Chancery.
Was it intended to stress the legal, binding force of the

[1] Above, p. 50.
[2] *Hemingi Chartularium*, vol. i, p. 287.

Survey by this brief title a generation before it got its popular nickname of Domesday?

There is little point in studying the Breviate in detail. The abbreviation was mechanically carried out, and can be grasped by a single example. On f. 166 of Great Domesday, the lands of the Abbey of Abingdon are set out, as *breve* No. 13 in the county of Gloucester. Abingdon held only one manor, described as follows:

[XIII] *Land of Saint Mary of Abingdon   In Gretestan Hundred*
The church of St. Mary of Abingdon holds Dubentone. There are there VII hides and a half.

[In demesne there are IIII ploughs and XIII villagers and VIII bordars with VIII ploughs. There are VI slaves and a mill of VI shillings.

In the time of King Edward it was worth XII pounds: now IX pounds. This manor used to pay geld in the time of King Edward.]

The Breviate text omits the words enclosed in square brackets, that is everything bar the tenant, the place, and the number of hides.

The special value of Heming's cartulary regarding Domesday springs from the fact that it is, like Domesday and Exon Domesday, an *original* source made by a church fully acquainted with the actual making of the Survey, close to events and presided over by a bishop who had been personally engaged in the process in 1086, and perhaps with the 'original returns' themselves in the early years of William II's reign. Its evidence agrees most exactly with that of our three Domesday manuscripts, and so pressing were the problems raised for Worcester by the Survey, that Heming included in his cartulary at least a couple of forged charters, purporting to belong to the tenth century.[1]

---

[1] The problems surrounding the Breviate are more fully discussed in *Herefordshire Domesday* (Pipe Roll Society, 1950). For the forgeries, see V. H. Galbraith, 'Notes on the Career of Samson, bishop of Worcester 1096–1112', *E.H.R.*, 1967.

VII

DOMESDAY BOOK IN THE THIRTEENTH AND FOURTEENTH CENTURIES

THE decisive testimony, then, of the 'Dialogue Concerning the Exchequer' is the best evidence of the importance of Domesday Book in the activities of the royal administration during the first century after its compilation. For its impact on the great 'honours' and 'fees' in the localities during the same period we have the tangled but copious remains of the local satellite surveys treated above. These miscellaneous records, it was found, supplied some, though not very much, first-hand evidence regarding the actual compilation of the Survey in 1086–7. But collectively they bear impressive witness to its practical influence upon local agrarian arrangements all over England. Though the evidence comes largely from ecclesiastical sources—cathedrals and monasteries—we can safely infer that every large landowner required a transcript of the Domesday entries relating to his own 'honour'; while the Pipe Rolls, surviving from 31 Henry I, and the Hereford Domesday suggest that the sheriffs and bailiffs in the counties must have also had the Domesday text in their offices.

This clear picture is, at first sight, confused by the early appearance in the twelfth century of Abbreviations of Domesday, whose very existence eluded Victorian scholars. Yet, these shortened versions are in fact the most conclusive proof of the abiding importance of the Survey, which set out in writing for the rest of the Middle Ages the basic pattern of English feudal society. The medieval mind in these centuries was dominated by vast, often universal, conceptions, in practice sadly limited by what we should call today their limited technology. Matthew Paris, the historian, and Thomas Walsingham a century later wrote huge universal histories, beginning with the Creation and extending to what was then 'the present day'. But both of them, with practical good sense, followed these works by at least two successive abbreviations, each more drastic than its predecessor. The theologians proceeded in the same way, and so too the lawyers, both canon and secular. There are thousands of such summaries in our libraries. So with Domesday Book, which seems to be a last-minute abbreviation of the huge local circuit returns, adopted at Winchester in the interests of practical utility. This process was carried further, as we have seen, within twenty years or so of 1086–7, by the omission of the manorial minutiae, already out of date. What mattered permanently was the personnel of the society set out in its county arrangement, together with the 'hidage' of each manor, and the ownership of the land.

When we pass from the twelfth into the thirteenth century, Domesday Book acquires a new kind of importance, as the primitive feudal structure of the 'new order' established by the Conquest is slowly transformed by the activities of the king's household into a parliamentary monarchy, in which by Edward III's reign sovereignty was almost divided between the Crown and its supporting magnates. In this creative process the largest factor was the development of the Common Law, which eventually was to put an end to feudalism altogether. In all this Domesday Book played an important part, and one which has no close European analogy. The government of the Norman kings had always revolved around the household offices of the Exchequer and the Chancery; and these in the thirteenth century developed into great offices of state, no longer within the royal household. Their procedure depended upon case law, and case law on the rise of a legal profession who relied heavily upon precedent. With the passage of time an elaborate legal system developed, whose records, still less than half explored, are preserved in the Public Record Office. In these and in the Year Books we can trace the influence of Domesday Book, the oldest and greatest book of precedents known to the royal bureaucracy.

The beginnings of the Common Law, stimulated by the genius of Henry II, can be dimly traced in the twelfth century; but it is only in the reign of King John that the evidence of its growth becomes detailed and consecutive. On his accession in 1199, by a famous ordinance,[1] he inaugurated the systematic preservation of copies of all the important documents issued by the royal administration. These Chancery Enrolments quite suddenly revolutionize the serious study of our history, as the central government rapidly extended the practice of 'enrolment' to other administrative activities, especially the records of the law courts. In the Curia Regis Rolls we find litigants claiming land *unde omnes antecessores sui fuerunt seisiti ut de feodo et jure et in dominio a conquestu Angliae.* High society was still essentially Norman, and pedigrees were traced back to the ancestors who came over with William the Conqueror—*qui venit ad conquestum Angliae.* Ecclesiastics and the king himself, equally relying upon Domesday Book, went still further back— to the time of King Edward (T.R.E.) or even earlier. To both lay and ecclesiastical landholders, every Old English right and custom—sac and soc, tol and theam and infangenetheof—was still a source of profit, and already the custom had grown up of buying from the king charters of *inspeximus* and *confirmamus* to perpetuate grants by earlier kings. To such a backward-looking but forward-moving society, Domesday Book was still a live record; and when, later, it came to lie behind the time of legal

---

[1] Rymer's *Foedera*, vol. i, p. 75.

memory, its evidence was still sought to solve problems
of tenure and service, and so it acquired ever-growing
authority and legality. Its text was scrutinized by each
successive generation of lawyers. Its evidence was vital
for settling the extent of the royal demesne, and under
Edward I for the extent of the forests, and all the puzzles
posed by his *Quo Warranto* inquiries, of which the monks
of Dunstable asserted that 'no good came'. So, in November 1300,[1] when the Exchequer was at York, Edward
ordered a search to be made of all the records, including
Domesday Book and the Red Book of the Exchequer,
touching the 'perambulation of the forests'. The Ward-
robe Book of the following year records payments to four
clerks for transcribing particulars from Domesday Book
and other payments for packing and dispatching the two
volumes of Domesday Book and other records to the king
at Lincoln.

By the fourteenth century the French language was
giving way to English as the upper-class vernacular, and
Domesday Book, though still growing in authority,
becoming more difficult to explain. So, in 12 Edward III[2]
the judges, puzzled to decide whether the lands of Roger
of Huntingfield were held of the king *ut de corona* or *ut de
baronia vel honore*, made their extracts from it and reported
*nescimus interpretationem facere nisi quatenus verba inde
sonant*, which may be roughly translated as 'We don't
quite know what it means, but this is what it says.'
Domesday was now behind the time of legal memory,
and three years later when cited to prove that land was
held of the king in chief, they argued that Domesday was
something personal to the king and not of record between
the parties.[3] It was none the less continually being quoted
by the administration, as for instance, in this extract from

---

[1] *Calendar of Chancery Warrants*, p. 120.
[2] *Cal. of Inquisitions Post Mortem*, vol. viii, p. 78.
[3] *quoddam secretum domini regis et non de recordo inter partes.* See *Year Books*
(Rolls Series), 14, 15 Edward III, pp. 346, 348.

the Issue Roll of 6 Edward III: 'To William de Boveye one of the clerks of the Exchequer, for extracting from Domesday Book the names of the towns noticed in the same book under the title of *Terra Regis* to be had for evidence in assessing the tallage newly to be assessed by the Council . . . 3s. 4d.'[1]

With the development of parliament in the fourteenth century, we find in the *Rotuli Parliamentorum* many references to Domesday in the petitions laid before it and in the judgements upon them. Many of these refer to the special status of villeins upon Ancient Demesne. When such a claim was made by tenants and rebuffed by their lord, Domesday was searched (*scrutato libro de Domesday*) and the evidence (generally unfavourable to the tenants) regarded as final. Difficult and often unanswerable questions were raised by these actions. In the parliament of 1334 the poor tenants of our lord the King in Archenfield[2] in the March of Wales, claimed to be excused from paying taxes with the other Ancient Demesne tenants on the evidence of an extract from Domesday Book which states that the men of Archenfield (then only half absorbed into the English shire system) rendered to the king only 40 sextars of honey, 20s. for eggs and 10s. *pro summagio*, that is for carriage; nor did they owe geld or any other customs except service in the king's army, if called upon. What exactly they made of this back reference to conditions in force two and a half centuries earlier we are not told. The king, as often, referred the petition to the Treasurer and Barons of the Exchequer to 'do right'. Many other such questions of fact were referred back to Domesday as in the very next year 1335[3] when the Earl Marshal and other March lords claimed that their seignories were outside the corpus of the county of Gloucester wherein the King's writ ran and sought to certify it from Domesday.

---

[1] Devon, *Issue Rolls*, p. 142.
[2] *Rolls of Parliament*, ii. 82.
[3] *Cal. of Miscellaneous Inquisitions* (Chancery), i, No. 1959.

Reliance by lay litigants upon Domesday Book in the fourteenth century, though not infrequent, has to be searched for in the records. For its employment by the Church, on the other hand, the material is far more abundant. By the end of the thirteenth century the best days of the Church were a thing of the past, and it was resolute in resisting change of any kind—doctrinal, administrative, or political. In every sphere of national life it was on the defensive, and its intransigence long retarded the normal civic development of the towns which had so actively developed on its demesne lands. Much of the evidence regarding these violent and frequent civic risings was carefully set out in Trenholme's *English Monastic Boroughs*.[1] These were either of royal foundation or, like Bury St. Edmunds, owned by mesne lords. In both cases the Church discouraged all attempts at self-government, but in general the towns who had any claim on Crown patronage or were of royal foundation, however remote, came off the better of the two classes. The citizens of mesne towns owned by the Church, says Trenholme, were in a constant state of political unrest from the close of the twelfth century which reached its climax in 1381. In origin, the Peasants' Revolt was a purely agrarian rising of peasants still legally serfs or bondmen, and therefore unfree. But in various parts of the country the citizens of monastic boroughs threw in their lot with their social inferiors, thanks to the brutal suppression of the first half of the century. Clerical intransigence towards all civic aspirations, in short, reached its climax just before the rising; it had crushed frequent revolts and, in the intervals between, fought long-drawn-out battles in the law courts. The Church relied on the evidence of its archives, of whatever date; and chief among these were the Domesday entries regarding what were then somewhat primitive, even rudimentary, conurbations.

[1] Norman M. Trenholme, *The English Monastic Boroughs* (Univ. of Missouri Studies, 1927).

Of this sad, yet heroic, period of civic struggle, much new evidence has come to light since Trenholme wrote, and more especially regarding the ancient abbey of Abingdon. It is clearly set out in an article by the late Mrs. Gabrielle Lambrick,[1] and is here briefly summarized for the vivid light it throws upon the employment of Domesday Book to counter town independence:

On the one side stood a powerful institution—for Abingdon was still one of the great English abbeys, of royal foundation and under royal patronage, whose head was a mitred abbot regularly summoned to Parliament, holding wide estates by barony and high privilege. On the other stood the townsmen of the little town of Abingdon, commercially successful, but of equivocal legal status, for their town was not a borough and they enjoyed no clear cut burghal rights.[2]

The struggle reached its climax in 1368, after much earlier futile litigation and violence; and its interest to us is twofold. First we note that it is not a simple dispute between a mesne town and its overlord, but a three-cornered affair in which the king's interest was divided between the parties. Secondly, it is plain that, in a mass of litigation far too complex even for summary here, the vital and fundamental document used by all sides was the entry regarding the Abbey of Abingdon in Berkshire Domesday.[3]

In the summer of 1368, then, the abbot of Abingdon was impeached before justices of oyer and terminer for levying certain dues in Abingdon, by extortion it was said, and for usurpation of royal privileges. The case dragged on until November 1372, when a judgement in parliament decided that the abbot was to be restored to full possession of the town and any who felt 'unduly aggrieved', were to find their remedy at common law.

In defence, the abbot might have pleaded a charter of

---

[1] 'G. Lambrick, 'The Impeachment of the Abbot of Abingdon in 1368', E.H.R., 1967.
[2] Ibid., p. 250.   [3] D.B. I, f. 58 b 1 (Berkshire).

King Edred in 955, which, though spurious, might have served the purpose. But it may be that this charter had perished in the burning and looting during the earlier riots of 1327. However that may be, the abbot's case stood firmly on the evidence of Domesday Book, which, roughly translated, was as follows:

The Abbey holds Bertune in demesne. T.R.E. it answered for 60 hides. Now for 40. There is land for 40 ploughs. In demesne are 3 ploughs and 64 villani and 36 bordars with 34 ploughs, and 10 merchants living before the gate of the church render 40d. and in Bertune 2 slaves and 24 *coliberti* and 2 mills worth 40s. and 5 fish ponds worth 15s. and 4d. and 20 acres of meadow and 15s. of pasture and 2 mills in the abbot's church unvalued. T.R.E. it was worth £20, and afterwards and now £40.[1]

The weakness of this evidence needs no demonstration, since it fails to mention the very existence of the town of Abingdon. It is silently included within the Abbey's demesne of the great manor of Barton, which formed the southern half of the Hundred of Hormer. The abbot's lawyers, Mrs. Lambrick pointed out, had to exercise great ingenuity in their efforts to circumvent this vital omission. They did their best with 'the ten merchants'; they asserted that the two mills and the fisheries were situated in the vill; and they concentrated upon the 24 *coliberti*, who they may have thought were the late eleventh-century lay servants of the abbey! They concluded that all these mills, fisheries, traders, and the mysterious *coliberti* must have made up the town of Abingdon, which in turn must have lain in the manor of Barton, since it was not mentioned elsewhere in Berkshire Domesday. These arguments were hotly contested, the Crown attorney being especially insistent. He denied that Abingdon was in Hormer Hundred, and asserted that Abingdon is and always was a town in itself and *unum grossum per se*, separate from the Hundred. We need not follow this further regarding castle guard at Windsor Castle, and the problems

[1] D.B. I, f. 58 b 1.

surrounding 'tolcestrepenyi'. Suffice it, that all sides were prepared to acknowledge the authority of the Domesday entry, the meaning of which none of the parties really understood. Indeed, the growth of the town of Abingdon in the three centuries since the Survey of 1086 still poses unanswerable questions to the trained medieval researcher today. But at least we can understand the frustration of the citizens of these monastic boroughs whose reasonable claims were ever more and more resisted by the joint forces of the Church and the Common Law until the sixteenth century. The growing prestige of Domesday Book in the law courts as the Middle Ages drew to their close was an unhealthy symptom of the waning of the Middle Ages, which grotesquely hindered national development in the fourteenth and fifteenth centuries. The world to which they gave way was the result, not so much of aristocratic or parliamentary action, as of irresistible social changes which in turn produced an economic revolution.

Of these social changes, the Peasants' Revolt is by far the most significant, for it was a massive and orderly protest against the legal serfdom of the majority of Englishmen, sustained so long only by the Church and the Common Law. It is therefore of importance to note that in 1381 Domesday was already proving itself a double-edged weapon, which could be used by high or low alike. A petition of the Commons in the Parliament of 1377[1] says that the villeins (*villani*) in various parts of England are purchasing in the King's Court exemplifications of those entries in Domesday Book relating to their manors, under colour of which they and their counsellors are retracting their due service. The petitioners 'remind the government of the aftermath of the French *Jacquerie* and hint darkly at the possibility of civil war or mass treason if a foreign enemy should land'. In the light of the events

---

[1] *Rolls of Parliament*, iii. 21b. Cf. May McKisack, *The Fourteenth Century* (1959), p. 338.

of 1381 nothing could better illustrate the morbid fear of the 'possessioners' regarding the peasants' actions which gave the lie to the fears of treason expressed in the petition. A Waltham Abbey writer,[1] who shared the fears of the Commons, wrote about this time:

In Domesday one can see what rights our manorial tenants ought to have *de jure*. I don't say what position they have at the present because by the long-suffering or negligence of lords and bailiffs and from the passage of time they enjoy a freer status now than they should ... to the disinheritance of the state of the Church and danger of the souls of those who ought, no matter what the difficulties to apply quickly some remedy. Such memoranda as these should not be let fall into the hands of unbelievers [*infidelium*] lest something sinister should come of it to the prejudice of our Church, and troubles and expense should thereby arise.

'The continuance and abundant evidence of Domesday as a work of practical reference for three or four centuries is, of course, only an example of the reliance on the past to meet the endlessly recurring difficulties that faced medieval government: but it is certainly the best example.'[2] Such overwhelming reliance on precedent, however, was not incompatible with administrative and political advance. Contrariwise, the solid foundations of the monarchical lay state of the future were laid in this period, and this secular progress continued into the first half of the fifteenth century. But in these centuries the evolution of the lay state was inextricably bound up with that of the Church, whose final allegiance to the sovereign papacy by the close of the thirteenth century acted as a powerful brake upon national development. This growing dichotomy between Church and State was not to be resolved until the reign of Elizabeth two and a half centuries later, and the slow but inevitable movement towards this consummation is superbly documented by the vast archives of the Public

[1] Harley MS. 391 (British Museum), f. 24.
[2] V. H. Galbraith, *Studies in the Public Records* (1948), p. 117, where the reader will find much of the material used above.

Record Office. Nor must we exaggerate the importance of Domesday Book in this period. There were many other precedent books, notably the Book of Fees and the Red Book of the Exchequer which carried an authority only second to it. But in this period Domesday Book was losing its original close connection with the Exchequer and acquiring a national provenance. Its prestige in the popular mind is shown by the increasing tendency to apply the nickname of 'Domesday' to local records of a specially authoritative kind. We encounter, for example, the 'Domesday' of Chester, the 'Domesday' of Newcastle, the 'Domesday' of St. Paul's. We even find the Red Book itself referred to as the 'Domesday of the Exchequer'. This pre-eminence of Domesday Book was in part due to its comprehensive character, but still more to its antiquity and to its radical character at the time when it was made—and it was made both as a record of the Anglo-Saxon past and as a lasting statement of a new feudal structure.

With the passing of the Middle Ages its practical importance declined, but it has remained ever since the most precious of our public records. Even in the sixteenth and seventeenth centuries it was a source of pride to its custodians in a period when our medieval archives were so carelessly treated. Thomas Powell in his *Repertorie of Records* (1631), describing the duties of the Deputy Chamberlain of the Exchequer, wrote:

> In searching the Booke of Domesdei is to be avoided, laying bare hands or moysture, upon the writing thereof and blotting.
>
> In copying of notes, out of the same booke of Domesdie, you must write it as neare as you can to the letter thereof, observing both the great letters and the poynts therein which are prickes with a pen: thus . . .

and he adds his attempt at a facsimile line of the manuscript. As a clerk in the Public Record Office after the First World War, I was still required to make certified office copies, minutely following Powell's instructions.

VIII

THE ANCIENT DEMESNE

THE foregoing chapters have provided evidence of the continuous connection of Domesday Book with both local and central administration—with the county sheriffs, with the Exchequer, the Chancery, and later still with the evolution of the Common Law. In this long period the judges who used it were sometimes uncertain of its very meaning,[1] so completely had the primitive feudal set-up of the eleventh century been transformed by the vigorous measures of the Angevin monarchy. Yet at no time was it forgotten, and in the fourteenth century it furnished evidence for the movements towards civic independence and the efforts of the agricultural workers to eradicate serfdom. We might almost say that, as the time gap lengthened, the less its evidence was understood, the more it was venerated. In this respect, its history was analogous to that of Magna Carta, the only other measure of equal prestige in our history. Professor Holt has called attention to the 'myth of Magna Carta' which arose in the time of Edward I, as it became a shibboleth in the struggles of that reign and later.[2] The less it actually 'meant', the more it was invoked. *Mutatis mutandis*, Domesday Book has suffered the same fate, but over a much longer period, since some of the medieval misunderstandings have continued to the present day. With one of these—the Royal Demesne— we are here concerned.

A century after its compilation, the king's officials, though continually referring to Domesday Book, had little or no knowledge of what really happened between

[1] Above, p. 115.   [2] *Magna Carta* (1965), p. 285.

1066 and 1086. Even the Treasurer who wrote the 'Dialogue concerning the Exchequer'[1] could only repeat what he had heard about it from Henry, bishop of Winchester, whose own career lay in the first half of the twelfth century. Nearly a century after the *Dialogus*, Henry Bracton and his colleagues were increasingly called upon to explain the text of Domesday, as well as to quote it. By the thirteenth century, Domesday lay behind the time of legal memory, though still evidence upon matters of fact. The judges were now repeatedly referring to Domesday to discover whether a particular manor had been part of the *Terra Regis* in 1086 or not. This, in turn, led them back to the problem of whether it had belonged to the Crown 'on the day when King Edward was alive and dead', that is 1066. In this way they were led to speculate on events between 1066 and 1087. But as historians they were very much out of their depth. Bracton, for instance, wrote: 'At the time of the Conquest there were free men holding their lands freely, and by free services or free customs. When they were ejected by stronger people, they came back and received the same lands to be held in villainage and by villain services, which were specified and certain.'[2] The passage is intended by Bracton to explain historically the varied species of unfree tenants on royal manors in his own day; and there is evidence in Domesday Book that something of the kind happened to many individuals. But as an explanation of a general process, it is no more than a guess based on oral tradition even less dependable than that of the writer of the *Dialogus* a century earlier. Both illustrate the growth of a myth, further developed by later lawyers prone to read back to Anglo-Saxon times later legal doctrines. One

---

[1] *Dialogus de Scaccario*, ed. C. Johnson, p. xx. 'His description of the settlement, parallel to Bracton's account of villein tenants in ancient demesne can hardly be regarded as history . . .'; and the same is true, Johnson insists, regarding the 'murder fine' and the historical explanation of blanch farm. But though his history may be discounted, 'it cannot be neglected'.

[2] Vinogradoff, *Villainage in England*, p. 121.

aspect of this process was the distinction thirteenth-century writers were drawing between the *Terra Regis* of 1087 and the concept of an Ancient Demesne antedating 1066.

To this matter of an Ancient Demesne of the Crown, Vinogradoff called attention in his *Villainage in England*,[1] and his views, much modified, were repeated by Maitland in the *History of English Law*.[2] The distinction, wrote Maitland, 'is hardly a matter of law: all the King's manors are the King's to give on what terms he pleases: still his ancient patrimony (viz. the manors held in demesne at King Edward's death) is regarded as more closely bound up with his office than are those mere windfalls which now and again come into his hands.'[3] Such is the classical doctrine of Ancient Demesne, and the nub of the problem it presents is thus set out by Maitland:

> On the ancient demesne there is a large class of persons whose economic and social position is much the same, if not quite the same, as that of the ordinary holders in villeinage, but who are very adequately protected by law or by custom which has all the force of law, in the enjoyment of their tenements. This protection is given to them by two remedies specially adapted to meet their case; the one is 'the little writ of right close according to the custom of the manor', the other is the writ of *Monstraverunt*.[4]

These are 'villein-socmen', and to the question 'How come that they enjoyed special privileges?' Vinogradoff gave this answer:

> Although there is no doubt that this tenure grew up and developed several of its peculiarities after the Conquest, *it had to fall back on Saxon times for its substance*, which may be described in few words—legal protection of the peasantry. The influence of Norman lawyers was exercised in shaping out certain actionable rights, the effect of conquest was to narrow to a particular class a protection originally conferred broadly, and the *action of Saxon tradition* was to supply a general stock of freedom and independent right, from which the

---

[1] pp. 89–127.   [2] *H.E.L.*, vol. i, pp. 383–406.
[3] Ibid., p. 383.   [4] Ibid., p. 385.

privileged condition of Norman times could draw its nourishment, if I may put it in that way. It would be idle now to discuss in what proportion *the Saxon influence on the side of freedom* has to be explained by the influx of men who had been originally owners of their lands, and what may be assigned to the contractual *character of Saxon tenant-right.* This subject must be left till we come to examine the evidence supplied by Saxon sources of information. *My present point is that the ancient demesne tenure of the Conquest is a remnant of the condition of things before the Conquest.*[1]

Maitland, profoundly influenced by Vinogradoff, but, as ever, more guarded, is in general agreement: 'All the evidence that we have conspires to tell us that there has been less change on these manors than elsewhere, and that the phenomenon before us is an unusual degree of conservatism.'[2] For Maitland, the king is the best of all landlords,[3] respecting custom rather than pursuing the 'enlightened self-interest' that was followed upon monastic estates.

For this doctrine of Ancient Demesne as a survival of things as they were 'on the day when King Edward was alive and dead', there is some evidence both in Little Domesday and in the Exon Domesday, of which both Vinogradoff and Maitland made much use.[4] But it also carried with it the highly unlikely hypothesis that between 1087 and Edward I's reign the king's lawyers had anticipated much modern research: that they had, in fact, gone behind the *Terra Regis* of the Survey to an Old English distinction between the king's Ancient Demesne and the more casual 'windfalls' in royal possession. However that may be, their conclusions have been flatly denied by the late Dr. R. Hoyt, an American scholar, in a closely argued book on *The Royal Demesne, 1066–1272.*[5] Inspired by C. H. McIlwain, and basing his arguments

---

[1] *Villainage in England* pp. 123–4. The italics are mine.
[2] *H.E.L.*, vol. i, p. 398.   [3] *D.B.B.*, p. 65.
[4] See Note at the end of this chapter.
[5] Dr. Hoyt's views are minutely set out in Chapters II and VI. For the 'Theory of Survival', see pp. 180 ff.

on the text of Domesday Book, Dr. Hoyt is first concerned to prove 'that (in the eleventh century) the administration of the realm is based upon no distinction, and
will nourish no distinction between an "ancient demesne"
of the crown and the private estates of the King'. The
phenomenon which puzzled Bracton was thus the creation
of the post-Conquest kings, more especially the Angevins,
intent upon the ruthless exploitation of royal demesne.
As for the villein-sokemen of the ancient demesne, they
are 'essentially villeins, who having direct access to the
financial and judicial system of an innovating and aggressive monarchy, are so benefited by that access that they
resemble sokemen'. The theory of ancient rights gradually
protected by writs contradicts the normal development of
common law, since new rights tend, in fact, to arise out
of writs governing procedure. Nor does Dr. Hoyt give
any weight at all to Vinogradoff's picture of a benevolent monarchy preserving on the royal demesne in the
thirteenth and fourteenth centuries 'the stock of freedom
which speaks of Saxon tradition'. The villein-sokemen of
the ancient demesne, unknown to Glanville in the twelfth
century, were a new thirteenth-century development and
the attempt to explain them as a historical survival was no
more than a Domesday myth.

Professor Hoyt's revolutionary views on Ancient
Demesne, though only a fragment of his researches, are
of special interest here since they sprang directly from
his study of Vinogradoff's *Villainage in England*, and the
History of English Law. But of even greater importance is
his whole approach to the subject of royal power in
England in the Middle Ages. Two desolating wars, with
their social consequences, have changed the 'climate of
opinion' regarding the very beginnings of our history,
and today the assumptions of nineteenth-century scholars
no longer seem valid to the rising generation. To the
nineteenth-century scholars the concept of evolution,

borrowed from the natural scientists, gave to the late classical and early Christian centuries an architectonic importance in national development, and their final verdicts depended on their feelings regarding the long Roman occupation and the Anglo-Saxon conquest of the fifth and sixth centuries. Undeterred by the lack of hard evidence, they envisaged English history as either the development of a slave society taken over from Roman Britain, or an idyllic prolongation of free village communities on the model of those described in Tacitus' *Germania*. The whole learned world was divided into 'Romanists' and the more liberal 'Germanists', though the weapons used by both sides were chiefly those of analogy and hypothesis.[1] Stubbs, Freeman, Vinogradoff, and Maitland were all ardent Liberals, believing in the survival of a 'stock of freedom' which survived the rise of strong monarchies and which accounted for the unique character of later English political institutions. In this war Vinogradoff in his *Growth of the Manor* (1904) was the last great master. Using an eclectic method he attempted to explain matters by allowing *some* force to Roman, some to Celtic, but still more to Germanic traditions. He had started in 1883 by studying English villainage in the late Middle Ages, worked backwards to Domesday Book, and, finally, harmonized his historical philosophy by a study of Celtic and Roman Britain. Both Vinogradoff and Maitland were basically jurists and lawyers writing history, and Vinogradoff's books in particular were inevitably tinged with the pro-German sentimentalism of continental Liberals. The contradictions which their naïve outlook gave rise to are still writ large in our standard textbooks today.

To turn from these masters of an earlier age to Professor Hoyt's *Royal Demesne* is to enter upon a new and more convincing world of thought; and his book is likely to form a watershed between the misguided approach of the

---

[1] See C. Petit-Dutaillis, *Studies . . . supplementary to Stubbs' Constitutional History*, vol. i, (1908), Chapter I.

nineteenth century, and the more limited, more positive, and more realistic—down-to-earth—outlook of the contemporary world. The outworn contests of Romanists and Germanists had no meaning for him, and without a blush he chose a new and later starting-point—that is Domesday Book itself, which is our earliest abundant source of hard evidence. His sole object was to understand 'the role and function of the English monarchy in medieval society', and this inquiry he reasonably concluded must start with the history of the royal demesne. Freed from any bias for or against the myth of a former paradise of free peasants, he brought out the immense potential of a monarchy which knew no strictly legal limitations. Instead of seeing the king as the best of all landlords, intent upon protecting his meanest subjects, he envisages an aristocratic, feudal, and even brutal process of royal aggression, developing in time into ruthless exploitation of what he most fully controlled—the royal demesne. No doubt his views will be challenged, as happens to all pioneers, but at least they cannot be ignored. The theory of the 'Mark System' antedated the French Revolution and, however watered down by Stubbs and the other 'Germanists', it or its ghost still haunts our text-books. But to the rising generation it may well appear as just a bit of 'non-history', the relic of a world-wide sentimental movement towards enfranchisement since 1789, unlikely to harmonize with the half-Marxist outlook of today.

NOTE ON ANCIENT DEMESNE[1]

The point at issue between Dr. Hoyt and Vinogradoff and Maitland recalls the mistaken belief that 'folk-land' meant land of the people, *ager publicus*, and was so described in the early editions of Stubbs's *Constitutional History*. Its true meaning was only discovered or rediscovered by Vinogradoff himself in the *E.H.R.*, 1893

[1] See p. 126 n. 5.

(pp. 1–17). As regards 'ancient demesne', it is no accident that the only hard evidence by which Maitland and Vinogradoff were able to support their sentimental interpretation is found in Volume II of Domesday and in Exon Domesday, both of which contain a more copious record of their circuits than that preserved in Volume I for the rest of England. Little Domesday (circuit VII) in several places speaks of manors as *de regno*, and in others of manors *de regione*.[1] Exon Domesday (circuit II) similarly mentions 'dominicatus regis *ad regnum pertinens*' (f. 83) and '*mansiones de comitatu*' (f. 106 b). On these Dr. Hoyt comments as follows:

> There is a real distinction implied by *regnum* and *regio*, but it must be sought in a different quarter. A fresh approach, which no one seems yet to have explored, is provided by assuming that the Domesday scribes meant exactly what they wrote when they used the word *regio*. Instead of a blunder for 'kingdom' or a crude expression of 'kingship' it simply means region, i.e. *provincia, scira* or *comitatus*. *Regio* has crept into the East Anglian text (Little Domesday) to express the same distinction brought out more fully by the *mansiones de comitatu* which are found in the Exon Domesday but nowhere else. In the East Anglian Domesday, *regnum* is opposed to *regio* just as in the south western Domesday *ad regnum* opposes *de comitatu*. This is a distinction between central and local administration, not a precocious political theory. *Mansiones de comitatu* and *maneria de regione* may have been meaningful phrases to the clerks of the Domesday circuits, but such manors are in fact *Terra Regis*, and the Domesday scribes at Winchester generally eliminated or ignored these local distinctions.[2]

Had the Victorian writers understood, as Dr. Hoyt did, the true nature of these two circuit returns, they would, I think, have been convinced, as I am, by his arguments. There are many other odd features about Exon and Volume II which patient research may yet solve.

---

[1] *D.B.B.*, p. 167 n. 2. J. H. Round, too, had noticed some of these (*F.E.*, p. 146) which he explained away as mere blunders, since he misconceived both the nature and origin of Little Domesday.

[2] *Royal Demesne*, p. 16.

IX

DOMESDAY STATISTICS

A. *Ellis's 'Abstract of Population'*

THE admirable Ellis in 1833 appended to his *Intro-duction* two indexes, arranged alphabetically, of the persons mentioned as holding land in Domesday Book: the first listing the persons or monasteries entered as holding in the time of Edward the Confessor and through later years anterior to 1087 (vol. ii, pp. 1–274); the second of under-tenants of lands at the formation of the Survey (pp. 275–416). These with the Indexes of Places (*locorum*) and of tenants-in-chief issued in 1811, as a separate volume, are still today, as they were then, the essential tools for studying Domesday Book. Merely to turn over the pages is to realize that no single lifetime could be long enough to master completely the vast bulk of statistics that Domesday records. Our debt, therefore, to Ellis far exceeds that owed to any other scholar. There has since been a great deal of further statistical research, notably in Professor Darby's giant *Domesday Geography*, but it is unlikely that Ellis's work will be superseded until, as now seems likely, the facts, in their entirety, are put through a computer; and this, of course, might revolutionize Domesday study.

Meanwhile, one cannot afford to neglect what is perhaps the most illuminating of all Ellis's services to Domesday Book, viz. the 'Abstract of the Population of the different counties of England' printed on pp. 419–514 in volume ii of his *Introduction*, and more especially to the *summary* of the numbers of every class of persons mentioned in the record with which it ends (pp. 511–14).

More than a hundred 'sorts of people' are mentioned; they vary from those (quite a number) mentioned only once or twice to the *villani* of whom Ellis recorded 108,407. It has been said that 'there are lies, d——d lies, and statistics'. Yet in spite of such warnings, all writers on the subject have at some point fallen back on Ellis's statistics to support their broader conclusions regarding Domesday Book. As statistics, it must be borne in mind, they leave much to be desired, since they summarize the figures not of a single but of at least seven different panels of royal commissioners or *legati*. Secondly, the returns depended on the facts supplied by thirty separate counties, each preserving immemorial differences of custom and outlook. And thirdly, that Volume II of Domesday contains a far more elaborate and detailed record than that preserved for the other twenty-seven counties. But they surely have significance when used to compare the relative numbers of the most numerous classes. Using round numbers, therefore, the larger categories are as follows:

Tenants-in-chief, including churches	1,400	
Under-tenants	8,000	
Burgesses	8,000	
Villani	108,000	
Bordarii[1]	82,600	200,000
Cotarii and Coscets	6,800	
Liberi homines[2]	12,000	
Priests	1,000	
Socmen[3]	23,000	
Servi	25,000	

Ellis's rough statistics have been used by all later scholars, and have deeply influenced their general conclusions regarding the social results of the Norman Conquest. In particular, Maitland analysed these figures in the first and third essays of his *Domesday Book and Beyond* (1897), and his broad conclusions are still held to be valid. First, he

---

[1] Including 'half-bordars' and 'poor bordars'.
[2] Including 'half-freemen'.   [3] Including 'half-socmen'.

decided that the *villani*, the *bordarii*, and the *cotarii* were but three species of the single genus—*villanus*—whom he described as 'the meanest of free men' (p. 31). Their combined total of about 200,000 thus accounted for more than half the recorded population. In striking contrast, the number of recorded *servi*, that is, of slaves or serfs, is a mere 25,000, which seemed to prove that in 1087 virtually the whole population were—nominally, at least—'free men'. He was, however, careful to define 'the meaning of freedom'. Some of his argument is invalidated by the common assumption of his day that the 'one mighty purpose of the Survey was the collection of geld', as well as by his views on 'Ancient Demesne', which he took over, or almost over, from Vinogradoff. Even so, his treatment of the *servi* and *villani* remains the most penetrating and witty[1] discussion of this baffling aspect of the Survey. He reminds us, for example, that there are 'hundreds of passages' which implicitly deny that the *villanus* is *liber homo*. He grasped, too, that the organization of the township was still 'of a most rudimentary kind'; and while not denying the existence of a 'communal sentiment' in the vill, insisted that it was 'if strong, still vague'. Nor did he fail to note that the 'open field system of agriculture' prevailed in villages under the control of a lord as well as in free villages. With all this in his mind, he confessed to deep misgivings regarding the 'definition of the freedom' of the *villanus* in Domesday Book: 'Therefore we shall not be surprised if in Domesday Book what we read of freedom, of free men, of free land is sadly obscure. Let us then observe, that the *villanus* both is and is not a free man.'[2] A depressing conclusion, but one which has never since been materially altered.

---

[1] e.g. 'the sons of a *villanus* who had but two oxen must have been under some temptation to wish that their father would get himself killed by a solvent thegn' (p. 44). The whole book is studded with such *bons mots*; cf. p. 142, 'not in any monstrous birth' do we find explanation of Domesday's '*semi-bos*', or, p. 439, of the drinking of beer, 'and who shall fathom that ocean'.

[2] *D.B.B.*, p. 43.

More than ten years later—after Maitland's death—Vinogradoff, characteristically summarizing a lengthy argument on the same question, concluded that villains in Domesday Book 'appear as a composite group in which both servile and free elements are clearly traceable', and that 'Domesday Book testifies to a rapid decay of the free classes'.[1]

Maitland's long argument on the effects of the Norman Conquest thus led him to the broad conclusion that 'we cannot treat either the legal or the economic history of the peasantry as a continuous whole: it is divided into two parts by the red thread of the Norman Conquest. That is a catastrophe . . . They (i.e. the villeins) were handed over to new lords, who were free in fact, if not in theory, to get out of them all that could be got without gross cruelty.'[2] A generation later his views were summarized by A. L. Poole, and still more directly expressed. It is, he considered, at least an open question whether the Domesday commissioners regarded the *villani* as free or unfree, but the rapid disappearance of the 25,000 *servi* marks the virtual disappearance of slavery, and was in fact 'the first great impetus which drove the peasantry on the downward path to serfdom'. The process was completed by the development of the Common Law after Henry II's reign: 'The lawyers are striving in the face of great difficulties to reduce the whole population into the simple classification of free or serf, *aut liberi aut servi*. Ultimately they were successful in degrading most of the peasants into a condition of serfdom.'[3] By the beginning of the fourteenth century, 'the greater half of the population', as Maitland put it,[4] were legal serfs, and so remained for

---

[1] *English Society in the Eleventh Century*, p. 470.   [2] *D.B.B.*, p. 60.

[3] A. L. Poole, *Obligations of Society* (1946), p. 13: a thoughtful and learned book in which the author used new evidence unknown to Vinogradoff and Maitland. His views are more generally set out in his *From Domesday Book to Magna Carta*, 1087–1216 (1951).

[4] *H.E.L.*, vol. i, p. 432. In recent books the tendency is to anglicize *villanus* as 'villain' in the twelfth century, and thenceforth as 'villein'.

two centuries. This 'serfdom', Maitland was careful to add, was both artificial and relative, in fact a 'juristic curiosity'. For the serf, the villein, though reckoned to be his lord's chattel, was virtually free against all save his lord. But this was exactly what rankled, for it meant that the serf could not seek any remedy against his lord in the common law courts. Nevertheless, Maitland had no doubt that the simplifying process of the lawyers greatly improved the position of the serf.

This view of the Norman Conquest as a legal catastrophe for the greater part of the population during the next four centuries, though now generally accepted, was revolutionary when it first appeared in the nineties of the last century, less than thirty years after Stubbs's *Constitutional History* (1873). Stubbs, who perhaps rightly distrusted lawyers and worked largely from the Chronicles took a very different view. The villain's legal disabilities against his lord were not, he believed, disadvantageous to him. In fact, 'under a fairly good lord, under a monastery or a college, the villein enjoyed immunities and security that might be envied by his superiors';[1] and he shrewdly doubted whether the word *villani* had during the twelfth century fully acquired the meaning of servitude which was attached to it by the later lawyers. His approach to the problem was more pragmatic, more rule of thumb, than that of Vinogradoff supported, though reluctantly, by Maitland; but like them he was deeply impressed by Ellis's Domesday statistics, which recorded no more than 25,000 *servi* in 1087. These figures, too, have been uppermost in the minds of more recent historians, faced with the problem of reconciling the three most progressive, constructive, and prosperous centuries of the Middle Ages with the simultaneous and systematic degradation of the majority of the population into legal serfdom. It informs A. L. Poole's view, cited above; and forty years

---

[1] *Constitutional History*, vol. i, pp. 466–7.

earlier, H. W. C. Davis in his *England under the Normans and Angevins*, 1066–1272—the most brilliant book of its age—affirmed that 'of all the contrasts which strike us in medieval life, none is so acute as that between the intellectual ferment in the upper classes and the oriental passivity of their inferiors'.[1] This was his 'last word', and later historians have been driven to postulate a sudden, new 'intellectual' ferment among the hitherto passive peasantry in the fourteenth century. Thus, Ellis's Domesday statistics, it would seem, have a great deal to answer for.

Are Ellis's statistics to be relied upon? Professor Carus-Wilson has taught us that the figures produced by medieval bureaucrats *can be* at times totally worthless; but the most searching scrutiny of the Survey over more than a century has led historians to an opposite conclusion. Edward Augustus Freeman, no doubt, went too far in asserting the infallibility of Domesday Book; but even Round, who delighted in finding errors in it, was convinced that the great masses of facts it records *regarding population* were scrupulously collected and, broadly speaking, accurate.[2] The fault then, if fault there be, must lie in wrong assumptions in the minds of the historians regarding their interpretation; and certainly the lame conclusion that it remains 'an open question' whether the Domesday commissioners believed the *villani* to be 'free' or 'unfree' points in this direction. The whole procedure of the great inquest was based upon a definite *questionnaire* requiring straight answers to straight questions; yet Vinogradoff and Maitland were unanimous in deciding that the Domesday *villanus* was both a free man and an unfree man! The conclusion, surely, so stated, is absurd.

May it not be that we have taken our lawyer-historians almost too seriously? The relevance of law to straight history increases rapidly as we approach the present, with

---

[1] p. 516; it is the last sentence of the book.
[2] But see below, p. 140.

its universal literacy and its 'mass media'. The further we go back the less its validity, so that for the still dark ages before the construction of the Common Law, it is more of a hindrance than a help for all but the élite in the class-conscious aristocratic society, which certainly antedates our earliest reliable source, Bede's *Ecclesiastical History*. In those illiterate and largely undocumented centuries Law, with a capital L, meant nothing to the peasantry. They were already governed by the squires and gentry of thousands of little villages, not yet 'manors'. They were the men who worked as *consuetudinarii* from dawn to dark on all but high days and holydays, following the immemorial processes of open-field agriculture through the revolving seasons. Their lives were governed by timeless custom varying from shire to shire, and their social horizon—at the widest—was bounded by the limits of their local Hundred. That they were, in theory, all *ceorls* with a *wergild* of 200*s*. is reasonably certain; but there is nothing in our sources to suggest that this had much meaning in Anglo-Saxon times or that their lives were much altered by the Conquest. The triple division of the population into earl, thegn, and ceorl of the Anglo-Saxon codes originated in the age of the *Volkerwanderung*, and long before 1066 the *Law* which they set out was relevant only to the prospering higher ranks of society. They looked no lower than the up-and-coming ceorl who had five hides of land etc., and might so become worthy of thegn-right. The life of the vast majority was outlined in the *Rectitudines singularum personarum*,[1] which distinguishes three categories of customary peasant life. To ask whether these three categories, which must have embraced more than half the population, were 'free' or not in the late eleventh century is thus to ask a non-historical, because an anachronistic, question.

The Conquest coincided with a great intellectual, religious, and economic awakening in Europe, which

[1] S.C., p. 89.

within a century was to transform the very meaning of
Law, and nowhere more so than in England where the
evolution of the centralized Common Law involved
a new dichotomy of the whole population into *aut liberi
aut servi*. If we approach the development of English
institutions in this empirical and pragmatic way, the
social process it presents is very different from that
depicted by the lawyer-historians of the Victorian age.
So far from seeing a calamitous descent of the mass of the
population into villainage, either from the ninth to the
eleventh centuries, or from 1066 to the thirteenth century,
we perceive a growing awareness by the peasantry of
their unhappy status of being merely customary tillers
of the soil, and we see them in ever-growing numbers
demanding freedom at common law. At no stage after the
Conquest were they either passive or oriental. The overworked oxherd in Aelfric's *Dialogue* is already unhappy
'quia non sum liber', because he is unfree, and a century
later villainage is seen by all men as 'without qualification
a degrading thing'.[1] In the second half of the twelfth
century *villani* are claiming in the king's court to be free
men; and their pedigrees show that already many of them
were unaware on which side of the line they fell.[2] By the
early thirteenth century they are finally integrated into
'society' by being at last sworn to arms; and we begin to
hear of the *communitas villae* as well as the *communitas
communitatum*, which was parliament. By Edward I's
reign, villeins are serving on juries side by side with free
men. Some of them already have their own seals; and by
the fourteenth century they issue their own charters.
What does this mean? In my view, it shows that the
peasantry—the 'free' and the 'unfree'—formed a single
fully integrated society in their villages and on their
manors.[3] In short, that before 1300 the upward thrust

[1] R. W. Southern, *The Making of the Middle Ages*, p. 106.
[2] Helen Cam, *Liberties and Communities in Medieval England* (1944), p. 134.
[3] G. Holmes, *The Later Middle Ages*, 1272–1485, (1962), p. 17, aptly quotes

they had so vigorously asserted for two centuries had rendered villainage a complete anachronism, sustained only by the unchanged hostility of their aristocratic superiors. The movement towards conscious 'freedom' was continuous from Anglo-Saxon times, becoming more sharply defined and transformed with the development of the Common Law, until by the year 1300 serfdom had become no longer defensible. There is massive evidence that the upper classes, and more especially the great churches, clung desperately to the hard line drawn by Bracton, Fleta, and the rest; and the anachronistic outrage of legal villeinage led inevitably to the very conservative Peasants' Revolt of 1381. Its occasion was no doubt the Black Death (1349) and its immediate consequences, but its fundamental cause lay in the process of social integration and ever-growing sophistication of the unprivileged masses. The evolution of English society, in many ways peculiar and even unique, was thus an expanding revelation across nearly 1,000 years, in the course of which the very meaning of Law and of 'Freedom', however slowly, changed like everything else. After 1381 by the intelligent action of lay landlords, the Church was quietly pushed aside and villeinage just withered away. How else can we explain the extraordinary fact that it was never formally abolished? All civilizations wither from the top downwards, and the English Middle Ages were no exception, though they spent a very long time a-dying. With them slowly decayed the legal importance of Domesday Book to the royal bureaucracy, only to be rediscovered and venerated as a part of history by the antiquaries of the seventeenth century. It was of this phase in Domesday studies that Round wrote: 'Wonderful are the things that people look for in the pages of the great Survey: I am always reminded of Mr. Secretary

from E. Miller's *The Abbey and Bishopric of Ely*, the biography of Stephen Puttock, a villein of this period, who 'was an important man in his village and a frequent member of inquest juries'.

Pepys writing for information as to what it contained "concerning the sea and the dominion thereof".[1]

B. *Maitland's 'Domesday Statistics'*

'The final result of the Inquest preserved in Domesday Book is a vast mass of statistics which has no parallel in the middle ages'; and the earliest reliable employment of this data is Ellis's 'Abstract of Population'. Nevertheless, Ellis's labours, however considerable, barely touched the fringe of the problem that these statistics present to the historian. Of this he was well aware, and so confined himself to recording the numbers of each class of the population mentioned in Domesday. Even this limited exercise was surrounded by many pitfalls which he discusses in his preface (pp. 419–24) and the copious notes to the totals in each county. More difficult and more questionable than the population figures are the many, many thousands of manorial particulars recorded: ploughs, money and food rents, woodland, pasture, pannage, mills, fish-ponds, hides, acres, geld and—most tricky of all—the money values (*valet, valuit*). From the first printing of Domesday Book this astonishing wealth of detail was minutely studied, county by county, by local historians, who ingenuously attributed to these statistics all the authority, and more, of a Victorian 'blue book' compiled by the civil service. The conception of Domesday Book as an 'infallible' authority was first seriously questioned by J. H. Round, who delighted in pointing out its omissions and its mistakes, in the destructive papers he wrote for the Domesday celebrations of 1886.[2] But his criticism was strictly confined to the errors made at Winchester in compiling Domesday Book from the more copious 'original returns'. No one as yet seriously questioned the validity of the 'facts' originally tendered to the circuit commissioners.

[1] *F.E.*, p. 230.   [2] *Domesday Studies*, ed. P. E. Dove.

Ellis apart, the first scholar to see the immense pos-
sibilities for future historians of Domesday statistics was
Maitland whose *Domesday Book and Beyond* (1897) is
still the most profound and imaginative treatise we have
on the Inquest of 1086. In it he deferred[1] unduly to the
dogmatic judgements of his two great contemporaries,
Round and Vinogradoff, but his intuitive grasp of the
total past was in a class apart, and he alone realized that
Domesday research was still in its infancy, when he
wrote (p. 520):

A century hence the student's materials will not be in the shape
he finds them now. In the first place, the substance of Domesday
Book will have been rearranged. Those villages and hundreds
which the Norman clerks tore into shreds will have been recon-
stituted and pictured in maps, for many men over all England will
have come within King William's spell, will have bowed themselves to him and become that man's men.

Forty years later these words inspired Professor Darby's
Domesday Geography,[2] which seeks to record in maps the
tangled statistics of Domesday Book, which Maitland
had first analysed in his *Domesday Book and Beyond*. Time
is already proving that Maitland's words on Domesday
statistics were prophetic. It would be a great mistake to
think of them as no more than a pious hope for the future.
They accurately summarize his own precocious excursus
into the field of statistical inquiry; and he thus justifies the
labour he spent on them:

Far be it from us to say that microscopic labour spent upon one
county or one hundred is wasted; but such work is apt to engender
theories which break down the moment they are carried outside
the district in which they had their origin. Well would it be if the
broad features of Domesday Book could be set out before us in a
series of statistical tables.

---

[1] He courteously postponed its publication until Round had published *Feudal
England*.
[2] Some of the difficulties it presents are discussed in my *M.D.B.*, pp. 214–22.

In this way he modestly introduces two elaborate tables of 'Statistics and Averages' (pp. 400–3), which deal with the whole country, and upon which the rest of the section was a commentary. This work is intended, he says, 'to be no more than a distant approach to truth. It will serve its end if it states the sort of figures that would be obtained by careful and leisurely *computers*, and therefore the sort of problems that have to be solved' (p. 407). Well, we now have the 'computers'—in a fullness even Maitland never foresaw—and whoever employs them must absorb the gist of Maitland's essay, difficult though it is.

There is nothing in the whole of Domesday literature so comprehensive as the essay's two concluding sections labelled 'Domesday Statistics' and 'Beyond (that is, Behind) Domesday'. As early as 1892 Maitland had written to Vinogradoff: 'Then as to Domesday, I have sweated over it and what I have written reeks of sweat— forgive the phrase—but owing to FP's. agnosticism— I am inclined to put it aside and leave D.B. to you and to Round. N.B. J.H.R. is in the field and you and he will be writing concurrently.'[1] *The History of English Law* appeared in 1895, with a chapter on the Anglo-Saxons, which Maitland 'did not like very much', by Frederick Pollock. This compelled Maitland to omit from the *H.E.L.* his own massive materials, which appeared two years later in *Domesday Book and Beyond*. The sequence is important, and strongly suggests that the two concluding sections of *Domesday Book and Beyond* were his 'last words' on the whole matter. In them he stood back, as it were, and, in the light of his own work, charted the progress made and the many teasing problems that Domesday statistics—in their entirety—still posed for future workers. In both sections he speaks for himself alone, but characteristically citing many other scholars, old and young, whose work time has proved to have been of permanent value: names like C. S. Taylor, Isaac

---

[1] Fifoot, *Letters*, no. 109.

Taylor, Eyton, Kemble, W. J. Corbett, Napier, Liebermann, and W. H. Stevenson.

Here, then, the whole spectrum of Domesday statistics
is analysed with insight and brevity. England, like Topsy,
had 'just growed', and still remained a congeries of widely
varying regions, each with its own age-long special
customs and usages. On all this confusion later conquests
had done little, if anything, to impose any kind of uniformity. The 'hide' was at once a unit of tax assessment
and an area of so many acres, which were equally un-
standardized. Similarly, the plough (*caruca*) and the plough
land (*carucata*) are not 'constants', and the only stability
they afford to the diffident arithmetician lies in 'certain
ratios'. In Leicestershire, 'we are driven to believe that
substantially the same piece of information is being conveyed to us, now in one, now in the other of the two
shapes, that in our eyes are dissimilar.'[1] In East Anglia, as
in Exon Domesday, where the records are so much more
comprehensive than in the rest of England, there are
special and formidable difficulties. Worst of all are the
uncertainties regarding the annual values (*valet, valuit*) of
the separate manors, which are at times manifestly bogus
(p. 473). 'Everywhere', Maitland concludes, 'we are
baffled by the make-believe of ancient finance.' The clear
moral is surely that the 'computerizing' of Domesday
statistics, to be significant, demands more expertise than
has yet been devised by students of the Inquest. Their
single common feature is that they are, in all circuits,
the answers to the same questionnaire, which precisely
defines the 'terms of reference' of the circuit *legati*. The
answers supplied show irreconcilable differences between
circuit and circuit, even between county and county. To
these problems Maitland applied a mathematical learning
that might well have puzzled a Senior Wrangler, and
reached no better conclusion than that the answers the

[1] *D.B.B.*, p. 421, and a footnote adds: 'To me it looks as if the variations were
due to a clerks's caprice'!

commissioners received to some of their questions 'were references not to existing agrarian facts but to a fiscal history which already lay in the past, and is now hopelessly obscure' (p. 473).

So much, then, Maitland proved to the hilt and no more. And his declared frustration compels the conclusion that the Domesday *legati* had recorded a hopeless jumble of outdated facts, many of which rested on no written records, and were mutually irreconcilable. To have ever thought otherwise most students today would regard as an anachronism; and the attempt to make Anglo-Saxon statistics work ended in a *reductio ad absurdum*. Yet Maitland still clung to the hope that though 'hopelessly obscure' they might somehow be explained; and the reason is not far to seek. For his whole argument is vitiated by two *a priori* assumptions. Of these, the first was his misguided belief that the one primary purpose of the Inquest 'was to tell the King's officers how much geld was due,[1] with a view to reassessing it on a more just and equitable basis'; and the second that the original hide, the 'large hide' was 120 acres,[2] which he held that Bede and the charters showed to be the typical allotment 'to each free family, to each house-father, to each tax payer (*tributarius*) one hide and no more, but no less' (p. 520). The first of these was taken over too modestly and too lightly from J. H. Round; and the second from Vinogradoff, anxious to establish the 'free origins' of English society. For neither of these preconceptions has research ever provided hard evidence. They are, in fact, just the wishful thinking of nineteenth-century 'Germanists', as unacceptable as the equally clear-cut Romanist theories

---

[1] This is most explicitly stated on p. 475, where he pictures the *legati*, by some ready process, 'doing sums' to make sense of statements like 'it gelded for 3 hides, 1 virgate and 1½ acres'. But he refers so often to the 'geld' in these pages as almost to suggest that he was unconsciously trying to convince himself of this Victorian dogma.

[2] Few, however, today will quarrel with Maitland's assertion that to the clerks of the Norman Exchequer in 1087 the hide was a hide of 120 acres.

of a fifth-century new society based upon the unfree farming arrangements of the Roman 'villa'. For both of these approaches to Anglo-Saxon history rest upon the failure of Victorian historians to understand the basic *aristocratic* structure of early medieval society.

Thus, Maitland's last words' on Domesday statistics, so far from proving any of these *a priori* assumptions, are the final demonstration of their inadequacy. To conclude, however correctly, that the *villanus* in Domesday Book was both a free man and an unfree man is a contradiction arising from the asking of a non-historical question. For this 'freedom' of barbarous peoples is different in kind from that of thirteenth-century common law, which was the result of many generations of silent social change. Between the one and the other stands the Domesday Inquest, which recorded the ever-varying customary regional dues of a still unintegrated England, but already gave a new and more limited meaning to the words *liber homo*. As for the great mass who were agricultural workers—the *villani*—all that could be said was that they were certainly not *servi*, but without thereby implying that they were 'free' in the eyes of their conquerors. That they were slowly *degraded* to villeinage in the next century is a misconception. Within a few years of the Inquest there is abundant evidence that judged by the later standards of common law they were already villeins, bondi, rustici, naifs, whose standing in society was little changed by the Conquest, for it was simply a matter of custom. The phrenetic zeal of our Germanist historians to discover 'elements of freedom' surviving the Conquest misrepresents the plain fact that the *villani* were without any known legal rights against their manorial lords before 1066 as in 1087. As the new vigour and wealth of the Norman kings transformed society and strengthened the monarchy, the *villani* strove energetically to share in the general betterment and, long before Bracton and Fleta had drawn the hard line between 'free' and 'unfree', had advanced socially to such a degree that all villeinage had become an anachronism. That the Peasants' Revolt did not occur till 1381 was due to the rigid persistence of the still aristocratic structure of society, increasingly supported by the machinery of the Common Law. By that time the Middle Ages were on their last legs, and villeinage, long since out of date, quietly withered away when it ceased to be profitable.

It would, however, be a mistake to regard Maitland's acute exposition of Domesday statistics as misguided effort. Far from it. No one before or since has studied them in such depth: and his final 'hope'—for it is no more—that they might some day throw new light on the dark pre-Conquest centuries, may well come about. But, if so, only when they are taken as we find them, objectively and without inherited preconceptions.

X

TOWNS, BOROUGHS, AND CITIES

THE serious study of Municipal History in England did not really begin until a century after the printing of Domesday Book in 1783; and this late start saved it from the dogmas and prejudices which so delayed progress in the manorial and agrarian field. Apart from Madox's *Firma Burgi* (1726), no book of importance appeared until the 1880s, which, as we look back today, appear as a 'golden age' of medieval research. A group of scholars, deeply influenced by the more advanced continental scholarship, then began to scrutinize our medieval towns. Outstanding among them were Charles Gross,[1] W. H. Stevenson,[2] Mary Bateson,[3] J. H. Round, and, of course, F. W. Maitland, the pre-eminent master in the study of town as also of manorial origins. The fruitful co-operation of these and other scholars enabled Maitland to synthesize and generalize in his *Domesday Book and Beyond* (1897) the process by which our earliest towns grew up, and to trace with authority in the *History of English Law* (1895) the gradual expansion of their 'liberties' from 'commonness' to 'corporateness'. His subtle insight and bold suggestion[4] laid the foundations of all later work, and nothing he ever wrote was more truly original. Nor must we overlook Maitland's more particular researches upon the city of Cambridge in his *Township and Borough* (1898), and, with Mary Bateson the admirable *Charters of the Borough of Cambridge* (1901).

[1] *The Gild Merchant* (1890).
[2] *Records of the Borough of Nottingham,* 5 vols. (1882–1900).
[3] *Records of the Borough of Leicester,* 3 vols. (1899–1905), and much else.
[4] Tait, *M.E.B.,* p. 339.

All modern thinking about medieval towns is based upon these four books.

Since Maitland's death in 1906, Municipal History in England has developed into a separate and flourishing branch of study engaging the whole energies of its devotees. Taught by George Unwin, historians have come to realize that across the centuries, the practice of voluntary association for the purposes of trade, has been a vital, perhaps the most vital, element in the growing sophistication of society which we designate as 'progress'. In this chapter, however, we are concerned only with the evidence up to and including Domesday Book, which in our books is no more than a first chapter and a dark one at that. We are therefore largely concerned with origins in a period for which we have no town charters that are not later forgeries, and are therefore dependent on the Anglo-Saxon laws and scraps from the literary sources. Nor must we forget that Domesday Book, which surveys most but not all the towns, cities, and boroughs in England, was compiled at a date when city life was making giant strides everywhere in Europe. So rapid was this advance that we must allow for great changes during the twenty years after the Norman Conquest, changes we cannot hope to measure today. But at least the evidence of Domesday, which marks the real beginning of our evidence for municipal history, demonstrates the *continuity* of town history during this troubled period; and corrects the more recent tendency to explain the origin of the *boroughs* in England in accordance with Pirenne's thesis regarding continental towns. In 1933 Professor C. Stephenson published his *Borough and Town* which maintained that the Anglo-Saxon borough has no real urban character and no burgage tenure, no free communal life; that it was, in short, a 'small, lifeless unit' until after the Conquest. This hasty view ignored the earlier research of Dr. Hemmeon in his *Burgage Tenure on England* (1914) and was finally corrected in James Tait's *Medieval English Borough*

(1936), which remains today the definitive summary of what can be safely inferred from Domesday about civic origins before 1066.

The Medieval English Borough (1936) marks beyond question the most important advance made in Domesday studies since Maitland wrote. Tait, it will be recalled, had criticized Maitland's 'garrison theory' when reviewing *Domesday Book and Beyond* in 1879, and in 1922 in his 'Study of Early Municipal History in England'[1] he had admirably surveyed the progress made before that date. In the remaining twenty years of his life, he devoted his whole energies to municipal history, devoting the first six chapters of his *The Medieval English Borough* to a minute and balanced scrutiny of the origins of town life. It was not easy reading; but remains the most judicious and clear-headed presentment of the valuable evidence by a scholar whose mastery of the text of the Survey exceeded that of either his predecessors or his contemporaries. However regrettable his long controversy with Stephenson, which at times was bitter, it sharply focused the points at issue between them, and so clarified his argument in this very difficult period.[2] The basic defect of the municipal historians, Tait decided, lay in their quest 'of a neat legal definition of the borough, applicable at all periods'. But the 'humble beginnings' of borough status antedated the Conquest, which marks no break in the continuity of the boroughs' development. Our burghal history was thus 'all one story'.

Tait's views, published more than thirty years ago, have gained general acceptance. Yet they are no more than a summary of conclusions to be drawn from the widely varying descriptions of individual towns, boroughs, and cities found in Domesday Book. Today these entries have been discussed very fully in the Domesday Book chapters of the *Victoria County History*. For nearly every county we

1 *Proceedings of the British Academy* (1922). Reprinted in *M.E.B.*, pp. 339–58.
2 e.g. pp. 130–8 concisely summarize Tait's broad conclusions up to 1066.

have now the translated text of the Survey, with long introductions of great scholarly merit. These demand close study, since they are for the most part the work of fine Domesday scholars, like Charles Johnson, F. M. Stenton, J. H. Round, and Tait himself. Taken together, these introductions supply us with a wealth of reliable fact, which, thanks to the Survey, is unrivalled for its date in any other country. For many of the larger towns, the ancient customs and renders in the 'time of King Edward' (T.R.E.) are set out in detail, followed by such developments as had taken place between 1066 and 1086.

Such is the basic material for the future study of the Domesday towns, and it is of high quality. In one respect, however, it fails us since all these works, including Maitland's, were written before the administrative process by which Domesday Book was compiled was brought to light. All these writers erroneously assumed that behind, that is prior to, both volumes of Domesday as well as Exon Domesday, lay a vast collection of Hundred Rolls at Winchester from which all these volumes had been compiled. J. H. Round, for instance, believed that Little Domesday was a 'first shot' at rearranging these (imaginary) geographical returns under the names of the tenants-in-chief:[1] and even Tait, as we shall see, was led astray. Future research upon the towns and boroughs must start from the fact that Little Domesday (Vol. II) is itself the solitary survivor of the seven or more circuit returns. All the others were epitomized in Great Domesday, and then, apparently, discarded, since no trace of them has ever come to light; and a comparison of the record of the towns in Little Domesday with the shortened narratives of the other circuits in Volume I, leaves us in no doubt that the surveying of the towns and boroughs posed large problems to the circuit *legati*, whose treatment varied markedly from circuit to circuit, and even from county to county.

[1] See above, pp. 7–8.

The fluctuating treatment of the towns, boroughs, and cities in the Survey is best explained by the fact that the 'terms of reference'[1] make no reference to their existence. These seem to envisage the country as a purely agricultural community; the wealth of which is recorded village by village or, more precisely, manor (or *mansio*) by manor. The first question the circuit *legati* put to the Hundred juries was 'What is the manor called?' and the second 'Who holds it?'. Later questions call for a return regarding the number of ploughs, the number of hides, of villagers, the extent of meadow, of pasture, of mills, fishponds, etc., none of which has much relevance to many of the larger urban communities. At first sight this extraordinary omission can be explained or explained away by the fact that the Old English administrative system treated the towns as either Hundreds in themselves, or parts of Hundreds whose financial potentialities were expounded by jurors of the Hundreds, some of which must have had an unusual civic basis, which we are often left to guess at. In this set-up, the towns, it can be argued, demanded no special procedure of their own. Yet, recollecting the extreme legal formalism of the 'sworn inquest' procedure, the omission of any guide-lines in the 'terms of reference' is highly surprising, and resulted in a striking contrast between the manorial descriptions and those of the towns. The former have, all over England, a set structure imposed by the terms of reference, while the descriptions of the towns, boroughs, and cities are so endlessly variable as to suggest that their juries were simply required to state their liberties and payments T.R.E., that is, in pre-Conquest days. Their answers were epitomized by the puzzled *legati* in their circuit returns and—one suspects—still further compressed in Volume I of Domesday. The entries for the larger towns, in particular, have no formal structure, and strongly suggest that, even as late as 1086, the Norman conquerors

[1] Above, p. 36.

were very ill-informed regarding the country they had conquered. It even, perhaps, explains the last-minute omission of both London and Winchester, which had already far advanced beyond the 'humble beginnings' of civic freedom, characteristic of so many of the Anglo-Saxon boroughs. Whatever the explanation of the omission, it reminds us that the wealth of England in 1086 sprang overwhelmingly from the ownership of land and the practice of farming. Town life and trade were still a very poor second string, though today their respective roles in the national economy have for a century or more become exactly reversed. No wonder, then, that Madox's *Firma Burgi* (1726) is the only serious book on borough finance until long after the reforms of the great commission on the towns set up in 1835. The boroughs remained from the thirteenth century, or earlier, special 'liberties', authorized by royal charter and outside the close control of the royal administration.

The difficulties encountered by the circuit *legati* were, it would appear, however faintly, recognized by whoever was responsible for the abbreviation of the circuit returns in Volume I of Domesday. There the descriptions of the larger towns are normally set out on the first folio of each county,[1] alongside the numbered list of tenants-in-chief. Tait in his *Medieval English Borough*[2] argued that the position of the towns so placed at the head of the county in Volume I implied their possession of 'separate courts, hundredal or other'. But for this assumption there is no hard evidence; and Volume II, our only 'original return', refutes his argument, since it records no such pride of place to any borough or city in Essex, Norfolk, or Suffolk. The compilers of the circuit returns, we may be sure, drew no such subtle distinctions. It may even be that the compiler of Volume I transferred the accounts of the larger towns to the first page of each county merely to facilitate reference to them amid the waste of village and

[1] Frontispiece.   [2] pp. 46, 49, 51, 55.

agricultural statistics. But more probably, I think, he was trying to remedy the unfortunate omission of instructions regarding the towns in the terms of reference, under which the *legati* acted.

This is a large problem, demanding a detailed analysis of every entry regarding the towns in Volume I of Domesday, county by county, which no one has as yet attempted. Here it must suffice to look briefly at the treatment accorded to the towns in Exon Domesday and Little Domesday, both of which antedated the compilation of Volume I.

1. *Exon Domesday (Circuit no. II)*

The initial procedure in this, as in all circuits, was guided by the verdicts of hundredal juries. It is, however, certain that no such *written* record as the I.C.C. for Cambridgeshire was ever made in this circuit. Contrariwise, it would seem that the evidence of the Hundreds was rearranged from the very start under the heading of royal demesne, followed by the fees and honours of the individual tenants-in-chief. We may safely make this deduction from the fact that neither Exon Domesday nor its epitome in Volume I (ff. 64 b–125) records the names of the Hundreds in which the villages, towns, boroughs, and cities were situated. It was an outstanding omission, indeed a blunder, which could not even be remedied at Winchester, and must have caused as much confusion in the Middle Ages as it has to modern historians, each of whom must make his own guess regarding the situation of every entry. Exon, is of course, only the preliminary draft of this circuit return of which large portions were not preserved. We cannot therefore safely argue from it; but when we turn to the epitome made in Volume I we find that while Cornwall (f. 120) and Somerset (f. 86) record no towns on their first folios, and Devonshire only one (Exeter, f. 100), Dorset provides on its first folio

(f. 75) short descriptions of four 'boroughs',[1] while Wiltshire contrives to mention on its first folio the names of no less than six 'boroughs'.[2] This first folio of Wiltshire is without doubt the most untidy, not to say slovenly, page in the whole of Great Domesday, and suggests that the Winchester compiler at the last minute altered his circuit return by transferring these—quite tiny—notices of boroughs from their original position to the first folio. This, of course, is only a guess but reminds us that the recording of towns in other circuits may well have varied, as here, from county to county, within the circuit. More certainly it proves that the attitude of the compiler of Volume I regarding the recording of boroughs and towns was at odds with that of the *legati* in circuit No. II.

Pending a full analysis, one notes that there is a wide variation all over the country regarding the size of the town entries in Volume I. Of certain towns, like Chester, Lincoln, and Oxford,[3] we have a wealth of detail regarding their ancient customs T.R.E., while of others we have almost none, and of some no entry at all. From this variation, the only safe inference is that the circuit *legati* were everywhere faced by problems arising from lack of instructions as to towns in their terms of reference. Nor, of course, can we ever be sure that the briefer notices are due to the Winchester compiler being required to jettison much of his material in the interests of brevity.

11. *Little Domesday, Volume II*

Here alone then, we are on firm ground, since it is itself the circuit return for East Anglia. It is of course drawn up on a far larger scale than the surviving abbreviations of all the other counties found in Volume I. Indeed,

---

[1] Dorchester, Bridport, Wareham, and Shaftesbury.

[2] Malmesbury, Wilton, Marlborough, Cricklade, Bath, and Salisbury. See Frontispiece and R. Welldon Finn, *Liber Exoniensis*, p. 146.

[3] For these see *S.C.*, pp. 103-7, where there is also a unique entry regarding the customs of the county of Berkshire.

it contains such a mass of astonishing detail about the holdings of small 'freemen' and 'sokemen', as well as regarding the towns, as to suggest most strongly that the circuit *legati* were altogether unaware that half or more of their so hardly gained information would, but for an accident, have been jettisoned by headquarters at Winchester. How, then, did the commissioners go to work?

The first county dealt with in Little Domesday is, as we should expect, Essex. The second is Norfolk, and the third Suffolk. In each of these successively, they must have collected the verdicts of the hundred juries, and at once converted them into schedules or *breves*—one for the king's lands, and one for each tenant-in-chief. In each county, after the fees of the tenants-in-chief there follows a section dealing with wrongful seizures of land, which is headed *invasiones super regem*. This procedure we suppose to have been followed in reinforced sessions of the county court; and when all this was done a written record made, of which the surviving manuscript was a 'fair copy'. The fact, which is not in doubt, is important, since it is our best proof that the circuit *legati* clearly believed that their 'local' return completed the Survey for these three counties. That, in the event, the contents of this volume, much abbreviated, were not entered in Volume I, was—we must suppose—because it arrived at Winchester too late for inclusion. And this assumption is perhaps borne out, not only by its tangled mass of detail about small free tenures, but also by the fact that while Essex was a normal southern county dealing in hides and virgates, both Norfolk and Suffolk were carucated areas, which farmed on a very different system, which must have puzzled the commissioners.[1] But what about the towns and boroughs? We note at once that the first page of each county is completely filled by a numbered list of tenants-in-chief, whose fees are then set out in detail; but in no

---

[1] For example, the unique system of geld assessment and collation by 'leets' is not even recorded for these two counties. Above, p. 60.

case is this list of land-holders accompanied, as is usual in
Volume I, by a description of the county town.[1] Their
treatment, which has been carefully summarized in J. H.
Round's Introduction to the Essex Domesday in the
Victoria County History,[2] can be summarized as follows:
There were twenty-one Hundreds in Essex, whose verdicts
were scrupulously recorded according to a clear order
beginning with Barstable and ending with Thurstable.
That no such document as the I.C.C. for Cambridgeshire
was ever made in East Anglia is proved by the fact that
two of these Hundreds—Dengie and Uttlesford—each
occurs twice in the series. This can only mean that these
two juries were recalled after their first appearance to
give further details.[3] This otherwise unvarying procedure,
however, was totally ignored in surveying the towns.
J. H. Round acutely noticed that the commissioners
solved the problem of the towns by according separate
treatment to the three largest towns in this circuit. In
Essex they relegated the elaborate survey of Colchester,
which fills three folios in the manuscript, to the very end
of their return, following the *invasiones super regem*.
Round wrote:[4]

It would be imagined from the list on the opening page of the
volume that the Survey of Essex closed with what it terms 'Invasiones'. But these on the contrary are followed by a long separate
survey of what is styled 'The Hundred of Colchester'. The position
here assigned to Colchester is well worthy of notice, for it contrasts
with that accorded to Ipswich and Norwich. The latter followed
by Yarmouth (Norfolk) and Thetford (Suffolk), is surveyed at the
end of the first division of the King's land in Norfolk (ff. 116–41),
while Ipswich is found at the end of all the King's land in Suffolk
(ff. 290). But the three towns have this in common; they are all
accorded separate treatment.

---

[1] See Frontispiece. The last section of the return dealing with the *invasiones
super regem* is not recorded on the first folio in any of the East Anglian counties.
[2] *V.C.H. Essex*, vol. i. pp. 333–426.
[3] *M.D.B.*, pp. 158 ff.
[4] *V.C.H. Essex*, vol. i, p. 414.

Such was the manner in which the *legati* dealt with the important towns in their circuit, and it suggests that the device followed in Great Domesday of recording important towns alongside the numbered list of 'the tenants-in-chief' was thought up by the Winchester abbreviator who discharged the responsible task of jettisoning a large part of the return before him. Whatever his motive in doing so, then, it was not shared by the man who actually surveyed the towns and boroughs, and we are left wondering how much of this copious and invaluable material would have still been preserved if Little Domesday had suffered the same fate as the returns of the other circuits.

There is, I think, no more vivid account of the Domesday towns than that found in Round's Essex Introduction. He points out that the great towns of Essex are Colchester, at its eastern extremity, and London which is beyond its western extremity; that not a single market is mentioned in Essex Domesday, while Chelmsford, which stands at the centre of the shire, does not even rank as a town. Colchester, already a town of importance, fills the last four folios of Essex county, including the names and payments made by 276 burgesses,[1] a class only found in one other Essex town—viz. Maldon. The whole entry, which bears the heading 'Hundred of Colchester', is thus a final addendum to the county return, of which it forms no integral part. It was characterized by 'tenurial heterogeneity', and clearly the *legati* were much puzzled what to do with it. Round even describes it as 'a separate survey'. He also shows that no legal distinction was yet drawn between 'cities' (*civitates*) and 'boroughs', since Norwich—a larger town than Colchester—is always called a *burgus*, while Colchester is variously described as a city and as a borough. Yet, somewhat strangely, Round adds that there are few traces of trade either at Colchester or Maldon even at a later date.

---

[1] A rare, and famous, reference which speaks of the burgesses holding land 'in common' is also discussed by Round, as it had been earlier by Maitland.

A comparison, then, of Little Domesday with the epitomes of the other circuit returns which alone survive for the rest of England in Volume I (Great Domesday) casts some doubt upon the conclusions of Victorian writers regarding the pre-Conquest boroughs. The Winchester compiler of Volume I certainly 'tidied up' his local circuit returns, and one seems to detect a better understanding on his part of the contrast the town descriptions presented to the agricultural statistics. But in so doing he may have intended more than merely to highlight the larger towns by setting out their descriptions on f. 1 of each county. We just do not know. A second point also must be stressed, viz. we do not know and can never know how much, if any, of the town material in the circuit returns was jettisoned in the compilation of Volume I. No valid comparisons therefore can be made between Volume I and Volume II, which are not in fact a single record, but belong to different stages of the Survey.

The towns, after all, had grown up piecemeal for centuries before 1066 in what until the tenth century had been a number of separate kingdoms. The wide differences between those more fully described in our record depended on age-long custom rather than on positive law. Nor must we take too seriously the references to the towns in the numerous codes of Anglo-Saxon law; which were, in general, counsels of perfection rather than legally enforced commands by the king's servants, as was soon the case after 1066. Finally, the circuit *legati* lacked the yardstick of precise procedure in dealing with the towns. They were entirely in the hands of their informants, and their chief interest lay in recording customary civic services and money payments.

Ellis, in his *General Introduction to Domesday* (1833) provided a valuable summary of the entries relating both to Cities and Burghs and Customs (vol. i, pp. 190–210) and Markets and Fairs (vol. i, pp. 248–57). For Ellis, writing before the reforming Commission of 1835, the towns were of merely antiquarian interest and presented no problems. He noticed, however, that in Domesday Book there were markets being held, and market tolls being taken, in many vills which were not of burghal rank.[1] Fifty years later Maitland referred to this passage, but by that time the problems raised by the Domesday towns had been narrowed down to one: the origin of the borough. 'What is it', wrote Maitland,[2] 'that makes a borough to be a borough? That is the problem that we desire to solve. It is a legal problem. We are not to ask why some places are thickly populated or why trade has flowed in this or that channel. We are to ask why certain vills are severed from other vills and are called boroughs.'

More recent writers, like Professor Carus-Wilson, are turning today to economic history, and so approaching Domesday problems from the wider angle of the growth of trade. This is a salutary development, and a corrective to narrow concentration upon the boroughs, whose later importance in the parliamentary system led our Victorian historians to read their history backwards. Although the whole history of English villages and towns is 'all one story', the law which decided burghal status was itself growing and changing almost beyond recognition until the close of the thirteenth century. The uncertain and fluctuating treatment of the Domesday boroughs, therefore, suggests that the question 'What makes an Anglo-Saxon borough to be a borough?' is something of an anachronism. The line of advance in further research lies in the proper understanding of the administrative process by which the Domesday record was compiled. And this in turn demands a new approach not to the printed volumes, but to the surviving originals. In 1783 Domesday was printed with meticulous care. It was as near to a facsimile as was then possible. Its very excellence misled our historians, and Maitland confessed, 'The one glimpse that I have had of the manuscript [i.e. of Vol. I] suggested

[1] Cf. *D.B.B.*, p. 193 n. 2.   [2] Ibid., p. 173.

to me (1) that the accounts of some of the boroughs were postscripts, and (2) that space was left for accounts of London and Winchester. The anatomy of the book deserves examination by an expert.'[1] There was, of course, already available the somewhat primitive photo-zincographed facsimile issued by the Ordnance Survey in 1862; but even this is utterly inadequate by modern standards, and the publication of a faithful facsimile of both volumes of Domesday and of Exon Domesday is the essential desideratum of contemporary scholarship. These volumes are bound to advance our knowledge; though even a facsimile can never quite replace recourse to the original manuscripts. In them alone lies the best hope of learning more about the puzzling problems which Domesday poses regarding towns and boroughs.

[1] *D.B.B.*, p. 178.

XI

THE GELD FALLACY AND SUMMARY

THIS survey of the progress of research upon Domesday Book since it was first printed in 1783 may
fittingly end, as it began, by recalling that it is our
earliest public record, which has never left official custody
since the Survey was made. It was William I's last major
undertaking, and its compilation marks with precision
the most important turning-point in the whole of our
recorded history. The new monarchy that made it possible
still reigns, and theoretically still rules the country; and
both our social establishment and our parliamentary and
legal system of government can be traced back with some
certainty to that reign. Behind 1066, as Maitland had
regretfully to admit, we still see our ancestors through a
glass darkly, still unable 'to think their thoughts, their
common thoughts about common things'. Nor have the
recent contributions of various ancillary disciplines—
philology, law, place-names, coinage, archaeology, and
pre-history—done very much to pierce this veil. The
concentrated research of more than a century was drawn
together and simultaneously expounded by three great
scholars: Vinogradoff, Maitland, and J. H. Round. Their
works form the firm foundation of all that has been
written since; and it is significant that the first two were
jurists and lawyers whose conclusions about all later
history were profoundly influenced and even shaped by
their Victorian preconceptions regarding society in the
dark centuries anterior to 1066. They were in fact
'Germanists' intent to find in Domesday Book evidence
that the beginnings of our later institutions lay in a 'free

village society' established by the Anglo-Saxon invaders.[1]
J. H. Round—the third great name, who learned history
from E. A. Freeman—was neither a 'Germanist' nor a
lawyer, but, at bottom, a genealogist of genius, who
worked in isolation and independently of the other two.
His contribution to Domesday research, which has
probably exceeded that of any other individual, has
hardly yet been fully assessed, for it was made not in
books but in scores of short papers, which were (more or
less) 'pulled together' in his *Feudal England* (1895).
Unlike the other two, Round never fully correlated his
discoveries, and in a long life saddened by grave illness,
made many enemies through his intolerance of error. So
far as his work overlapped that of Maitland and Vinogradoff, it is relevant to add that, of the three, he was the
first in the field, much of his most compelling work having
been produced in the eighties; and their thinking was
much shaped by his early discoveries, which have long
since passed into all our textbooks. Yet Maitland remains
today our most 'classical' writer on Domesday, as on the
whole subject of medieval law. His two eminent contemporaries have long since become no more than vital
sources to be studied only by specialists, while *The History
of English Law* and *Domesday Book and Beyond* still hold
the field of Domesday research.

Meanwhile in the seventy years since Maitland wrote,
the whole climate of scholarship has changed, and so
given a new slant to Domesday studies. Of this new
attitude, Dr. Hoyt's *Royal Demesne*, as we have seen,
is an outstanding example. Ignoring the half-mythical

[1] How completely such wishful thinking dominated Domesday studies in the
late nineteenth century is apparent from James Tait's review of *Domesday Book
and Beyond*, mentioned above (p. 9). Tait, who was then (1897) a young man
of thirty-five, began his long review as follows: 'The battle of the Romanists and
Germanists has raged fiercely since Fustel de Coulanges in France and Mr.
Seebohm in England threw their bomb into the Teutonic camp. For a time the
assailants carried all before them, but of late the Germanists, plucking up
courage, have examined the foundations of their citadel and convinced themselves that they have successfully resisted the mines of the besiegers.'

beginnings of English society, he makes Domesday Book his starting-point, and in so doing gives a very new look indeed to his history of the three following centuries. This is the more remarkable as his work was directly inspired by Vinogradoff's elaborate treatment of Ancient Demesne published in his first book on English Villainage in 1892. That he comes to such very different conclusions is due in part to mere lapse of time, but also to the progress made by Tout, Poole, and others in administrative history. Since Maitland wrote, their work has profoundly changed the modern attitude toward royal bureaucracy, shattering the sentimental nineteenth-century conception of Norman kingship. The conquest of England is today regarded as just a part of Norman 'expansion', closely comparable with the conquest of Southern Italy, and the later state founded in Antioch. It was in fact a new beginning, and for this reason, perhaps, the most theoretically complete 'feudal' state in the whole of Europe, despite the efforts made to suggest unbroken continuity with the old English monarchy it had ousted. By 1085 the period of turmoil was over, and William sought for what we should now call the details of its 'economic wealth', with an eye to future exploitation of his legal revenues. He was already well aware of the military service 'by which his chief followers held their fees' and honours, for all these vital matters were no more than an extension of relations already operative in Normandy. The time had come to disentangle and codify all those immemorial non-feudal customs and renders which the Old English king had annually received from his sheriffs in the counties. With all this recorded in writing, he would know the financial facts regarding both his own 'royal demesne' and the 'honours' of his tenants-in-chief. So strengthened, he could hope to make realistic assessments of the 'reliefs', the 'wardship' payments, the 'fines', the 'marriages', and suchlike payments on which a feudal king depended.

In the intricate muddle of Norman finance, the collection of the geld played a big part, partly because it was a direct and universal levy from all estates, partly because it could be—or at least was—fixed at whatever figure the king decided, sometimes 2*s*., sometimes 4*s*., sometimes 6*s*. on 'the hide'. For William exacted it, like all other *customary* renders, from the moment of the Conquest. It was therefore no mere 'drop in the bucket', but it was still far from being a major source of revenue. Actually, we are very poorly informed regarding the geld, and the only reason we hear about it at all is because it bore so hardly on the peasants; for when the rate was stepped up to 6*s*. on each hide, the king, as a sop, gave exemption to the 'demesne' lands of his tenants-in-chief. But the complaints of the poor in that aristocratic world, though aired in the Anglo-Saxon Chronicle, counted for nothing, and geld lingered on for another century as just another, and waning, 'custom' collected by the county sheriffs and forwarded in cash annually to the royal treasury at Winchester. The sole authority for the collection of such payments, whether called *census*, *scot*, or *geld*, was iron custom, and there is no evidence at all that the Survey was made by a beneficent king anxious to correct outdated assessments. When the immemorial pre-Conquest assessment of geld became hopelessly inept, the remedy applied was to lower the total number of hides liable in any such Hundred by a constant fraction, say by a quarter or a fifth; and we have several examples in Cambridgeshire. Exemption from the payment of geld was only granted as a privilege by the Crown to individual landowners. Another point of interest must be mentioned, viz. that the word *Danegeld* appears only once in the whole of Domesday Book (Vol. I, f. 337 b 2), and even there in close juxtaposition with the word *geltum*. The implication this carries is that to the Norman circuit *legati* it carried no sense of historic meaning, or recollection of its origin. The king's officials knew it just as 'geld'—so much on the 'hide'—unless it carried special exemption. Had it only been collected once or twice in William's reign, as Stubbs taught, it would surely have borne its older name, as it did in the twelfth century, when the conquerors had learned more of the history of the England they had conquered. Nor must we forget the single 'geld roll' of some year in the seventies which has survived[1] and is drawn up in English. Nothing could do more to prove that the geld was a normal, annual collection, made by the officers of the Hundred, passed on to the sheriff, and finally sent in with his whole account to the Treasury.

Such, very briefly, are the hard facts known about the 'geld', and they make nonsense of the view that the one primary purpose of the Survey was the 'quest of geld'. The terms of reference under which the circuit *legati* acted do not even mention geld. The origins of hidage assessment lie too far back in history to be fully understood, and scholars still argue the merits of the 'Tribal Hidage' and the 'Burghal hidage'. But upon the almost antediluvian attribution of so many hides to each village or estate depended the whole system of village life and organization, both financial and military. The first question asked in 1086 was 'Who holds the manor?', and the second 'How many hides does it answer for?' Both questions were necessary to identify the thousands of manors about which the juries of the Hundred were asked for particulars. Sometimes, as in Northamptonshire, the juries answered simply 'There are X hides', the payment of geld being taken for granted; in other counties they remarked more specifically 'There are X hides *ad geltum*'. It was just another necessary statistic to be noted, along with ploughs, pasture, villains, mills, etc. And what about an intention to reassess it.? The very idea is an anachronism for the date. But we can go further than this, thanks to the survival in Exon Domesday of an *inquisitio geldi*, the sole purpose of which was to catch land-holders

[1] *Anglo-Saxon Charters*, ed. A. J. Robertson, pp. 230–6. Cf. p. 92 above.'

who had long been 'concealing' hides. This was rapidly carried out, and the information gained used in the Domesday Survey. The government, in short, wanted to extort the last penny. We assume today that the *inquisitio geldi* was carried out in all circuits—but we have no proof. However that may be, Exon Domesday, as it were, puts the geld inquisition in its true perspective, viz. as a rapid preliminary to the Survey to catch defaulters. But there is no doubt that these south-west 'geld accounts', based on an *inquisitio geldi*, are partly responsible for the modern obsession of scholars with the idea of geld reassessment. In fact, the geld was never reassessed, nor could have been by any such inquiry as that of 1086–7. In Norfolk and Suffolk, for example, the wholly unique organization of geld payment by 'leets' is not even recorded.[1]

It is thus necessary to examine more closely the unanimous, but untenable thesis of our three Victorian historians regarding the overwhelming importance of geld in the Survey of 1086–7. As early as 1886 Round commented upon the 'obsolete assessment of the geld'[2] and added, 'it is clear that one of the main objects of the Domesday Survey itself was to obtain "a register" of real, as distinct from assessed value', giving as his proof: 'This view is confirmed and illustrated by the great Carucage of 1198 more than a century after Domesday'. Maitland unwisely accepted Round's dictum, reducing it almost to absurdity when he wrote:

All the lands, all the land holders of England may be brought before us but we are told only of such facts, such rights, such legal relationships as bear on the actual or potential payment of geld. True, that some minor purposes may be achieved by the king's commissioners, though the quest for geld is their one main object. . . . Our record is no register of title, it is no feodary, it is no costumal, it is no rent roll; it is a tax book, a geld book.[3]

[1] *The Kalendar of Abbot Samson*, ed. R. H. C. Davis.
[2] P. E. Dove (ed.), *Domesday Studies*, vol. i, p. 116, Round's essay 'Danegeld and the Finance of Domesday' is still the most exhaustive and learned discussion of the geld known to me.   [3] *D.B.B.*, p. 5.

With all this Vinogradoff was in full agreement:

The Survey, to which we owe our most precious information in regard to English institutions and society, is mainly directed towards ascertaining the data for the imposition and repartition of the geld. It became the invaluable cadastre which we know because such a cadastre was wanted by the officers of the King's Exchequer to check returns and to effect necessary modifications of the tax.[1]

The same view is repeated in the Domesday section of each county in the *Victoria County History*, and in countless textbooks and bibliographies; and by many scholars writing today. Is there not something inherently improbable in the assumption that the greatest military aristocracy in Europe was dragged into the county courts and forced to reveal its total financial resources in order to reassess an ancient customary render, paid for the most part by the agricultural labourers, and no more than a fraction of the royal revenue? The very notion is contradicted by the arrangement of both the circuit returns and Domesday Book itself under the fees of the tenants-in-chief, whereby the village and manors were, as Maitland said, 'torn apart'. The whole thinking behind the Survey was Norman, and therefore feudal; while its execution was governed by the deep-seated Old English administrative machinery of county, Hundred, and village.

Such unanimity of error is extremely rare on any major historical question, and therefore requires explanation. To whom do we owe this oldest dogma of Domesday interpretation? The credit is usually attributed to Round, whose *Feudal England* (1895) begins with the now famous sentence: 'The true key to the Domesday Survey, and to the system of land assessment it records, is found in the *Inquisitio Comitatus Cantabrigiensis*.' But before Round had ever heard of the I.C.C., first published in 1876, he had learned from E. A. Freeman, who had written: 'The payment and non-payment of the geld is a matter which appears on every page of the Survey; and it is perhaps not

[1] *English Society in the Eleventh Century*, p. 141.

too much to say that the formal immediate cause of making the Survey was to secure its full and fair assessment.' From whom did Freeman obtain this view? The answer, as we so often find, is that he got it from Ellis's *Introduction* (1833). Ellis wrote: 'By this Survey the Conqueror was enabled to fix the proportion of Danegeld on the property of each land holder' (vol. i, p. 350); and again (vol. ii, p. 420): 'The Domesday Survey is but a partial Register. It was not intended to be a record of population further than was required for ascertaining the geld.' And Ellis in turn took over his view from Mr. Philip Carteret Webb's *A Short Account of Danegeld, with some further particulars relating to William the Conqueror's Survey* (1756). In Round's hands 'this precious evidence' revealed 'the whole *modus operandi* of the Great Survey'. Up to a point he was right, for the I.C.C. is the solitary remaining evidence of the initial *procedure* followed by the circuit *legati*. But, as so often, the discovery was pushed too far by Round's hasty assumption that the circuit returns to Winchester were drawn up in the manner of the I.C.C., that is, as Hundred Rolls, systematically describing each village, Hundred by Hundred. From this too lightly adopted thesis Round could never escape, not even when faced by the irreconcilable evidence of Exon Domesday, and it woefully misled Domesday scholarship for more than half a century. For even Freeman in a long appendix on Domesday[1] had already grasped that 'the second volume of the Exchequer Domesday, the Exon Domesday, and the Inquisitio Eliensis seem, as I have said in the text, to be the original record of the Survey itself, which appears in the first volume of the Exchequer Domesday in an abridged shape'. And all three volumes were already drawn up feudally, i.e. under the names of the tenants-in-chief. But 'Mr. Freeman,' wrote Round, 'most ardent of Domesday students, knew nothing of this precious evidence', viz. the I.C.C., lately printed by

---

[1] *Norman Conquest*, vol. v, Appendix on Domesday, p. 735.

N. E. S. A. Hamilton; and malice clouded Round's judgement, as later in his strictures upon Hubert Hall's *Red Book of the Exchequer.*

The results of Round's error are still with us today, for Maitland calamitously accepted his interpretation; but here we must realize that Round's misunderstanding of the actual process of the making of Domesday Book was due initially to his acceptance of the still older error of regarding the motive behind the Survey as simply or predominantly due to 'the search for geld'. By the middle of the eighteenth century, when Webb[1] wrote, we can already trace the beginnings of critical scholarship upon pre-Reformation history, and it has long been assumed that Webb's article was the *terminus a quo* of this almost universal fallacy. However, thanks to Professor McKisack we can now carry it back almost two centuries earlier, viz. to Arthur Agarde (1540–1615), Deputy-Chamberlain of the Exchequer, who wrote a little treatise on Domesday, and was, perhaps, the earliest pioneer of research upon it as a mere historical curiosity. 'Anticipating Maitland', she writes,[2] 'by some three hundred years, he connects the survey with Danegeld: its purpose, he hazards, was to enable the King to learn how much every town, vill and hamlet was bound to pay.' And so at last we discover that the basic conclusion of Victorian research on Domesday is that advanced nearly four centuries ago in the darkest age of Tudor ignorance of the Middle Ages. Domesday Book, having finally ceased to be of any practical use to the daily administration, was more and more venerated by antiquaries as a landmark in our history. By the sixteenth century the dark ages were remembered as a sequence of tall stories, beginning with the Trojan origin of the English nation, then Boadicea, continuing through Alfred and the Cakes (from Asser!) to Canute and the Waves, and

---

[1] P. C. Webb, *A short Account of Danegeld with some further particulars relating to William the Conqueror's Survey* (1756).

[2] May McKisack, *Medieval History in the Tudor Age* (1971), p. 86.

so to the Danegeld and the house-carls, and finally to Domesday Book, which was then apt to be regarded as a re-edition of a survey called 'Liber de Wintonia', originally made by King Alfred. It was through this prehistoric jungle of confused national memory that Ellis had to hack his way in his famous *Introduction*; and by and large, he did it very well, struggling with great names like that of Sir William Blackstone, who believed that 'feudalism' was not *imposed* by the Conqueror but nationally and freely adopted by the general assembly of the whole realm in 1085![1] These and similar crudities of thought were gradually overcome after the printing of Domesday Book in 1783, but throughout the nineteenth century the conception of the eleventh-century monarchy remained a complete anachronism, and the motives attributed to William I supposed a political outlook not very different from that of Queen Victoria and Mr. Gladstone, and more especially regarding 'national finance'. In his chapter on Domesday Statistics Maitland attributed both a knowledge and a machinery of ordering revenue wildly at variance with the then half-barbarous state of society. But at least he was aware as no other man in his generation that the solution of our problem then lay, as it still lies, far ahead.

Maitland was right. All history is an attempt to understand the feelings and the thoughts of folk in the past. It is no more than an ideal, at any rate in the Middle Ages, and research advances in proportion to the historian's capacity to escape from logical preconceptions of his own society, by which he is imprisoned. The story of Domesday research is repeated in all fields. The events will not of themselves teach us much until we can speak the thoughts of the men responsible for them. There can be no 'last word', and anachronism will persist, possibly increasingly, as times recede into the past. Nor must we forget that our scholarship, as it is called, has lagged

[1] Ellis, *General Introduction*, vol. i, p. 16.

sadly behind that of continental Europe. Behind the imaginative expounders, like Maitland, and the brilliant 'discoverers', like Round, are a whole army of experts, among whom W. H. Stevenson was pre-eminent, each bringing his special skill. Round failed utterly to explain the separate provenance of our three original manuscripts; and though he persuaded—we might almost say bullied— his generation into believing him, he landed the learned world in a self-contradictory explanation of the Survey, which was briefly as follows. The purpose of the Survey was to fix and reassess the geld. Therefore, the original returns were a vast series of Hundred Rolls, since geld was both fixed and collected by the local divisions of the Hundred. At Winchester these vital documents were jettisoned (for no trace of them has ever been found) in favour of a 'feudal' summary arranged under the names of tenants-in-chief, from which the geld was never, nor could have been, reassessed or repartioned. Great Domesday thus became an unexplained afterthought, or at best a complete change of plan. That this was nonsense is sufficiently proved by the contemporary literary evidence; and its futility was finally displayed in Round's own lifetime. For when the *Victoria County History* was published, Round was called upon to write the historical introduction to the Domesday section for Somerset. The publishers naturally worked from the fuller text presented in Exon Domesday, and Round (together with his pupils) was driven to ignore its evidence, and to affirm that its date, its nature, and its evidence were beyond human explanation. This was in 1913, and he could do no less, since he had ostentatiously omitted Exon from his Pedigree of Domesday manuscripts in 1895.[1] By this time there were already some doubts,[2] and Stevenson had already printed Robert of Hereford's testimony in the *English Historical Review*.[3] A new interpretation of the Survey was required,

[1] *F.E.*, p. 146.   [2] F. H. Baring in *E.H.R.*, 1912, p. 309.
[3] *E.H.R.*, 1907, p. 74.

which I put forward in the *E.H.R.* in two articles (1942 and 1950). In *Domesday Re-Bound* published by the Public Record Office in 1954, one can observe the editors struggling vainly to harmonize the evidence of the valuable Appendices contributed by Miss Daphne Gifford with the outworn conclusions of the nineteenth century. Finally, the whole argument was set out in full in *The Making of Domesday Book* (1961). To that the reader is referred for the full proof of the process by which the greatest of all medieval administrative records was so rapidly produced.

How it was all done is not the end of Domesday research. Rather it is only the first step towards understanding the true purpose of the Survey. It was the logical and inevitable consequence of the Norman Conquest, designed to harness the wealth of England to the new contractual system of feudal baronies: in short, a written record of the new order, as seen through Norman eyes. It owes its preservation to the stroke of genius by which, sacrificing formal completeness to practical utility, the Treasury officials at Winchester jettisoned so much of the hardly gained information. Its guiding principle, viz. 'that all land is held in the last resort by the king', 'came to us in the guise of a quiet assumption: no law forced it upon the conquered country; no law was necessary; in Normandy lands were held of the Duke, the Duke again held of the king; of course it was the same in England; no other system was conceivable.'[1] The object of the Survey was thus to assess the total resources of the Royal Demesne and of some hundreds of baronies, held by the tenants-in-chief, and this could only be done by showing the wealth of both parties in each county; and so by using the pre-Conquest administrative machinery of villages and Hundreds. For centuries to come, then, England became perhaps the most 'feudal' country in Europe, but its administration followed the ancient pattern. The full

[1] F. W. Maitland, *The Constitutional History of England*, (1909), p. 155.

implications of this revolution eluded the Victorian historians, who hopelessly confused the necessary procedural use of hundred juries with its sole purpose, which was from the outset to summarize the total assets of the new feudal aristocracy. Hence their grave error in jumping to the conclusion that the circuit returns were a huge collection of Hundred Rolls, a view which suggested the still graver fallacy that the Survey's object was to reassess the ancient geld. This view, in turn, suggested that Domesday Book was a momentary measure, with a very restricted object. And this in turn has had disastrous consequences upon the writing of our later administrative history.[1]

Meanwhile, younger historians are now busy revising the whole Victorian presentation of both our foreign history and England's importance in Europe in the Middle Ages. In the nineteenth century the pre-eminent political standing of Great Britain in world affairs gave rise to an insularity of treatment no longer acceptable. European history was treated as revolving around England in relation to which foreign countries appeared as satellites. The kings of France were seen as dim background figures, while the personalities of their opposite numbers in England were carefully analysed and their individual contributions to England's future minutely assessed in the light of later events. Stubbs, the great master, disliking the French, saw medieval Europe through German eyes; and this gave lasting value to his

---

[1] For example, even the late Helen Cam (*The Hundred and the Hundred Rolls* (1930), p. 195), our safest guide to the royal administration of Edward I, was misled by her experts into regarding his Ragman rolls as intended to become a second Domesday Book. 'Edward I's Domesday Book', she wrote, 'was never completed, and the rats have devoured the greater part of the material from which it might have been made.' In fact Edward I's numerous commissions after the year 1274 were made by the justices' clerks, and belong to a far later stage of administrative development. There is no reason to believe that they were ever intended to form a second Domesday Book which their sheer bulk would, in any case, have rendered impossible, as well as futile.

treatment of Old English history. He very properly attached importance to the role of its ancient monarchy, and, even more notably, did full justice to its peculiar monastic church. But his acount of the Norman Conquest was much impaired by his hesitations concerning the introduction and early development of that most French, as well as Norman, institution which he already called 'the feudal system'. J. H. Round, in his only polite controversy, for he respected as well as feared the bishop, won a long battle of words by his convincing 'Introduction of Knight Service into England',[1] which began, he rightly insisted, the day after the battle of Hastings. To this Stubbs gave grudging acknowledgement in the later editions of his *Constitutional History*; but, for Stubbs, the French conquerors were all but Englishmen by the time of Henry II, whom he credited with the design of eliminating feudalism's baneful influence.

The President of St. John's College, Oxford, in a recent book[2] which broadly surveys the European Middle Ages, sees the whole process in a very different light. For him, from the twelfth century onwards, the whole European states system—its chivalry, its literature, and its sanctity—revolved around France; and by its close England, 'mesmerised by the prospect of continental glory', was 'an integral but *subordinate* part of a European order' dominated by France. All Europe admired the gaiety of France and its buoyant and confident attitude. It was universally described as 'douce' and 'belle', and its kings 'enjoyed the advantage of an unfailing favourable public opinion', for they were 'the sole heirs to the sacred kingship of the early middle ages'. French medieval history thus presents a striking contrast to that of England, whose kings throughout the Middle Ages—much as in Germany in the past century—lived under the strain of frantic but unavailing efforts at foreign conquest.

[1] *F.E.*, pp. 225 ff.
[2] R. W. Southern, *Medieval Humanism and Other Studies* (1970).

This revolutionary shift of opinion is very relevant to
Domesday research, so much of which was done in the
shadow of Victorian nationalism. Dr. Southern takes up
the story in the twelfth century, but the superior prestige
of the French monarchy, if not yet so potent as a century
later, was already a fact in 1066, and our histories overrate
the importance of both England and Normandy at that
date. William was no more than a feudatory of the French
king, labouring under the disability of illegitimacy, and
the invasion of England just one more freebooting ad-
venture, which, against the odds, succeeded. His world
centred upon France, and his motives were the lure of
England's great wealth and—even more important—the
potential asset of its ancient monarchy in his struggle with
the French monarchy. As a relative of King Aethelred,
he had some claim to succeed the childless Edward,
but mere heredity counted for little in the eleventh
century, when each king dated his reign, not from the
death of his predecessor, but from his election by the
Witan and immediate coronation thereafter. So the reign
of Harold, though it barely covered a year, was none the
less a fact which could not be ignored. True, William in
1066 had the blessing of the Pope, who regarded Archbishop Stigand as schismatic. But the Pope, like England,
counted for less at that date than a century later. So
William's first act after the 'miracle' of the battle of
Hastings in September was to ravage the southern
counties and then, but only after three months, compel
the Witan to crown him king on Christmas Day. Thus
his real claim to succeed rested only on his victory at
Hastings; and the protracted, if intermittent, resistance
of the English for some years thereafter made it necessary
to discover a valid reason for his aggression. So arose the
absurd pretext that Edward the Confessor had, in 1051,
conceded the succession to the throne fifteen years before
he died, and the cock-and-bull story of Harold's perfidy
in ?1064, after swearing future allegiance to William.

This travesty of history, depicted in the Bayeux tapestry, is a striking proof of the lengths to which Norman clerical propaganda would go to justify the accomplished fact of his conquest. And it needs hardly to be said that there is no contemporary, i.e. pre-1066, evidence for a word of it. In fact a very early charter of King William, written in English and issued in 1067, before Norman rule had been set up in the south-west, grants to Regenbald, his priest and first chancellor, land in Wiltshire 'as fully and freely as it belonged to "Harald Kinge".[1] It is one of William's earliest recorded acts as king of England, and manifestly antedates the invention of the Bayeux tapestry story. When, twenty years later, the Survey appeared, Harold was never accorded in it the title of king,[2] and the reign itself, which was a fact, was treated as a non-event. An air of further verisimilitude was imparted by tracing back the legal possession of every manor in England 'to the day on which King Edward was alive and dead', a formula so endlessly repeated that it was cut down to three letters, T.R.E. The Normans, then, having first made up their story, stuck to it in Domesday and so into the next century. As late as 1161, King Edward was formerly pronounced to be a saint by the papacy, the Normans having quickly hitched their wagon to the sentimental cult of Edward as a saint which their oppression gave rise to so early among the conquered English.

An earlier stage, before the full story was elaborated, was conveyed by William's great seal, the first he ever had. It copied that of King Edward, but with a significant

---

[1] *Regesta* i, no. 9; Round, *F.E.*, p. 422. Once only is it said in D.B. that Harlod *reigned* (I, f. 38 a 2), while Edward the Confessor is twice mentioned as 'gloriosus rex', a portent of his coming sanctity.

[2] Cf. Ellis, *Introduction*, vol. i, pp. 303, 311. He is uniformly referred to as *comes Haroldus* in both volumes, as also in the I.C.C. and Exon Domesday. The only exception occurs in Herefordshire (I, f. 180 a 1) where we read 'Heraldus tenebat quando mortuus fuit (at Hastings), when the scribe (? in decency) omitted the *comes*. William similarly is only once said to have conquered (*conquisivit*) England. Domesday generally says 'postquam venit in Angliam', and Harold is referred to as 'the usurper' (*invasor*).

difference. Edward's seal had shown him as Basileus 'in majesty' on both sides, while on that of King William, the king was, on the reverse, seated, like his would-be predecessor in majesty; but on the obverse, as duke of Normandy, he was pictured on horseback, as a warrior in chain-mail. This proclaimed merely to the world that the duke of Normandy had added England to his duchy. But on the seal of William II, the separateness of Normandy was abandoned. The king in majesty was shown on the obverse, while the mounted warrior became the reverse, with the words *dux Normannorum* on the encircling lettering. Already then by 1087 the embarrassment of Harold's reign had been overcome by Norman propaganda and the story of Harold as merely the 'invader' of the kingdom for less than a year had passed into official history. He is still apt to be omitted from the list of English kings in our textbooks.[1]

Had the story told in the Bayeux tapestry been in accordance with the known facts in 1066, William would have dated his reign from the day on which Edward the Confessor was alive and dead. But this he never did, not even in Domesday, the making of which is correctly attributed to 1086, in the twentieth year of his reign, that is from his coronation. Stenton was careful to point out that 'the continuity of the English administrative system was preserved in Harold's time'.[2] The fact is attested by his issue of 'a voluminous currency'; and though only a single royal writ from his writing office has survived, he

---

[1] The whole story is elaborately told in Professor Douglas's biography of William the Conqueror (1964). The author, though inclined to deny that William ever visited England in 1051 (p. 169), still accepts the view that Edward bequeathed his kingdom to William. Similarly, though he accepts the story of the tapestry and later French historians about Harold's oath, he is careful to qualify it all by the words 'as it would seem' (p. 175). He also discusses (p. 251) William's claim to succeed by 'hereditary right', citing a charter to the Abbey of Jumièges describing him as 'Ego Wuillelmus Normanniae dominus jure hereditario Anglorum patrie effectus sum Basileus' (Round, *Calendar of Documents Preserved in France*, 918–1206, vol. i (1899), p. 526).

[2] *Anglo-Saxon England*, p. 573.

must have had a royal secretariat to issue his vernacular charters. Without it, Harold's administration could not have functioned. It would therefore seem possible that on his seal the king was first depicted, on the reverse, as a mounted warrior. It would also account for the hesitating —almost ambiguous—wording of the legend on William's seal, viz. on the *obverse*: HOC NORMANNORUM WILLELMUM NOSCE PATRONUM: and on the *reverse*: HOC ANGLIS REGEM SIGNO FATEARIS EUNDEM. Yet, so successful has the propaganda story proved, that historians tend to suppose that Harold never had a great seal, simply because no trace of it remains. The late Florence Harmer, for example, discussed at some length the question whether Regenbald, to whom Edward the Confessor had accorded the status of a diocesan bishop, presided over the writing office successively of Edward and William I. She wrote:

Regenbald appears in Domesday as a wealthy landowner holding lands and churches in several shires, but although he stood high in the favour of Edward and William I—both of whom issued writs in his favour—he was never raised to the episcopate as were other king's priests. Can we suppose that his services in the king's writing office were too valuable to be dispensed with? Or did some obstacle stand in the way of his advancement?[1]

The fact of Harold's reign is here completely ignored; and the answer to her questions is perhaps that Regenbald was the *de facto* chancellor not only of Edward and of William but *also* during the intervening reign of Harold. This is at least likely, since at that period the new king normally continued the chancellor of his predecessor in office for the first year or so of his reign. The makers of the Bayeux tapestry knew better than this, and as a matter of course depicted Harold as Rex (king); but tried to have it both ways by a preface intended to

[1] F. E. Harmer, *Anglo-Saxon Writs* (1952), p. 211.

show that he was a *perjured* king. For this preface there is no hard evidence; and while its origins lie in the period immediately following William's coronation, its consummation is set forth in detail in Domesday, which treats the reign of Harold as though it had never occurred.[1]

It is difficult, as always in the Middle Ages, to understand from the purely clerical narratives at our disposal, the outlook of the ruthless military adventurers who actually dictated the course of events. They were the only real realists in an age of turmoil, and there is no reason to think that either they or their successors were deceived by the sham façade of legality erected to justify the Norman Conquest. Contrariwise, they never scrupled to remind their sovereign that it was only by their support he had 'brought it off'.[2] In this awareness lay the abiding flaw in later English kingship. For William's followers, though not for either the Church or the unprivileged, English feudalism was a new beginning. English kingship was shorn of the half-mystic authority which surrounded its beginnings in France. England became, in this aspect, the most completely feudal state in Europe; and this best explains the English kings' imperfect grip on their military supporters for centuries to come—on which Dr. Southern lays such emphasis.

It has already been suggested above that both William I and his feudatories were still poorly acquainted with the 'foreign' niceties of English tenure and taxation in 1085. For these in the Survey they relied upon the knowledge of

---

[1] Tout, *Chapters*, vol. vi, p. 1, lists Regenbald as William I's first 'chancellor in 1067; C. R. Cheney (*Handbook of British Chronology*, p. 81) begins with Herfast? 1068; but both appear to accept Wyon's statement (*Great Seals* (1887), p. 5) that Harold never even had a great seal. Miss Robertson (*Anglo-Saxon Charters*, p. 471) and H. W. C. Davis (*Regesta*) similarly ignore Harold's reign. It was Round who first called attention to the mention of Harold as king, and printed the text of the vital writ in his 'Regenbald, Priest and Chancellor' (*F.E.*, p. 421).

[2] It is—and most significantly—the assumption of the Battle Abbey Chronicler: e.g. pp. 87, 88.

their English subjects, even down to the reeve, the priest, and six villagers mentioned in the terms of reference. Already the interests of the great Norman magnates, as well as their sovereign, lay as much in France as in England, a fact borne out by the slow emergence of the chief justiciarship, an office necessitated by the long absences of the kings abroad. The secondary position that England held in royal policy left the field clear for officials like Ranulf Flambard or Roger, bishop of Salisbury to concentrate upon purely English justice and finance, and so to evolve the uniquely centralized bureaucracy of England and its common law. This process of administrative development was speeded up by the foreign ambitions of the Norman and Angevin kings, which proved more and more costly. Their policy can be summed up by the proverbial *ivstitia est magnum emolumentum*, and it has been well described as 'self-government by the king's command'. It is the common delusion of economic historians that medieval barons had the same grip of the details of finance as modern American millionaires. This notion is belied by the fact that their education was wholly different from that of the churchmen, who were the normal medieval administrative class. The knightly code was that of Courtesy and Chivalry, and the more it decayed as the centuries passed, the greater was the insistence of the baronial class, including their kings, that their sole business was that of fighting. It required the Wars of the Roses to replace them by a more civilized upper class. But we must not exaggerate by antedating this tendency. All our Norman and Angevin kings—bar Stephen—were outstanding personalities, and queer ones at that; and two of them in particular, Henry II and John, were personally and closely interested in English administration. None the less, they were far more deeply involved with, and intent upon, continental adventures. The French kings of the same period—bar Philip Augustus—were personally hardly their equals. But, as

Dr. Southern explains, in that aristocratic and backward-looking age, they had no need to be. Supported by their half-mystic past, the French kings for centuries were 'the cynosure of neighbouring eyes' and the central figures in the European order. On them world affairs centred, while in England the development of bureaucracy was left to clerical officials. In this way the Domesday Survey continued to influence English administration in the thirteenth and fourteenth centuries.

Thus the propaganda regarding William I's false claim to the English throne won in the end, for it sustained the continuity of English administrative development from Anglo-Saxon times. Without it, the substantial contribution of pre-Conquest conditions to later history would never have occurred: Domesday Book might never have been written, and England might have developed on much the same lines as did France. Dr. Southern, then, is not wide of the mark in regarding the elaborate administrative measures which revolutionized English justice in the twelfth century as a 'token not of royal interest but of the lack of it'. The tangled and forbidding texts of Liebermann's *Gesetze*, which demonstrate the unbroken evolution of our later law from pre-Conquest arrangements, were the concern of royal officials whose measures paved the way for the later English parliamentary constitution. *Quod facit per alios facit per se*; and the credit for all this activity belongs to our Norman and Angevin kings. Yet it is noteworthy that the same administrative pressures were not exerted upon their continental possessions, which ended, up, as they began, entirely French.

The new credulity of much modern research is, today, an increasing menace. The whole narrative of the Norman Conquest in the chronicles lacks hard contemporary evidence, and stands self-condemned, as so often in the Middle Ages, by being grossly overladen with trivial corroborative detail. The acid test lies in the endless

variety of this detail in successive versions.[1] William of
Poitiers, William of Jumièges, the Bayeux tapestry,
Eadmer, William of Malmesbury, Orderic Vitalis, and
Wace all differ from one another in pretended particulars,
while in full agreement about Harold's oath. In those
days one meets constantly with fact that is already passing
into fiction, and thence, not seldom into romance. We
shall never know how far this process had gone in the
story of Harold's 'perfidy', or how different were the
facts upon which, no doubt, it was founded.[2]

We, in turn, are admittedly thrown back upon specu-
lation. But it may well prove that, as scholars more and
more write their history forwards instead of backwards,
the Domesday Survey, as the logical outcome of the
Conquest twenty years later, will gain a deeper contemporary significance than historians have so far accorded to
it. But already we shall not go too far in maintaining,
first, the supreme importance William attached to his
bogus claim to have been the chosen heir to the English
crown, fifteen years before the Confessor's death; and
secondly, that the imperfect hold of later English kings
upon the allegiance of their barons goes right back to
their awareness that the feudal settlement described in
the pages of Domesday Book was based upon an initial
lie. William's title to the throne was no better than that of
Harold—indeed it was worse—and what really happened
on the death of Edward the Confessor is recorded in
the contemporary 'Life' of Edward the Confessor.[3] It
knows nothing of the later propaganda story so graphically

[1] William of Malmesbury, who had the root of the matter in him as a historian,
is careful to introduce the Harold story with the words 'ferunt quidam' (vol. i,
p. 279).

[2] It goes back, as so much else, to Freeman's *Norman Conquest*. Freeman, for
whom all chronicles, regardless of date, were 'evidence', decided reluctantly and
against his own better judgement that the Harold story could not be ignored. In
his third volume (Appendix V) he devoted thirty pages to it as 'one of the most
perplexing questions in all history'.

[3] *The Life of King Edward the Confessor*, ed. Frank Barlow (Nelson's Medieval
Texts, 1962).

depicted in the Bayeux tapestry; and this in turn necessitated in Domesday Book the assumption that Harold
had really never 'reigned' at all. By the end of the reign
the royal administration worked rigidly on this assumption, and so pretended that there had never been a 'terra
regis', a royal demesne, during Harold's reign. His
single writ (K.C.D. 976) proves the existence of a
chancery and a seal; and that no others have survived is
at least partly explained by the denial he had ever truly
'reigned', which was implicit in the systematic confirmation of privileges in William's charters from 'the day on
which King Edward was alive and dead'. But the precise
form of Harold's seal still remains anyone's guess.

APPENDIX

EXON DOMESDAY

List of Contents

f. 72   Isti sunt illi hundreti in Cornugallia [Geld account for
         Cornwall].

   75   Isti sunt hundreti de Sumerseta [Geld acount for Somer-
         set].

   83   Dominicatus Regis ad Regnum Pertinens in Devonescira.

   88 b Dominicatus Regis in Sumerseta.

   93   Dominicatus Regis in Devenesira.

   99   Terrae Regis Dominicae in Cornugalliae.

  103   Terra Regis Quas tenuit Godwinus Comes. Et filii eius
         in Sumerseta.

  108   Terra Mahillis Reginae in Devonesira.

  111 b Terrae Mathildis Reginae in Cornugallia.

  113   Terra Editdae Reginae in Sumerseta.

  116   Terra Quae Fuit Vluardi Wite in Sumerseta.

  117   Terrae Sancti Petri Essecestrensis Aecclesie in Devene-
         scira.

  121   Terra Episcopi Constantiensis in Devenescira.

  136 b Terra Episcopi Constantiensis in Summersetae Syra.

  154   Terrae Osmundi Episcopi in Summerseta.

  156   Terra Gisonis Episcopi in Summerseta.

  161   Terra Abbatis Glastingheberiensis in Devenesira.

  173 b Terra Episcopi Wintoniensis in Sumerseta.

  177   Terrae Abbatis Tavestochensis aecclesiae in Devenesira.

  180 b Terra Abbatis Tavestochensis in Cornugallia.

  182   Terrae Abbatis Bulfestrensis aecclesiae in Devenescira.

  184   Terra Abbatis Horthonensis in Devenescira.

  185   Terra Sancti Petri de Bada in Sumerseta.

  188   Terrae Sancti Petri Michilinensis Aecclaesiae. [In
         Somerset].

  191   Terra Sancti Petri Adeliniensis aecclesiae in Sumerseta.

f. 193 b Terra Abbatissae Sancti Edwardi in Somerseta.

  194   Terrae Aecclesiarum Quae Date Sunt Sanctis in elemosina.

  196   Terra Quae Datae Sunt Sanctis in Elemosina in Summer-
         seta.

  199   Terra Episcopi Exoniensis in Cornugalliae.

202   Terrae Sancti Petrochi de Cornugallia.

205 b Sancti Achebranni Terra.

206   Terrae Sancti Probi. de Cornugallia.
      Terra Sancti Carentochi.

206 b Terrae Sancti Stephani in Cornugallia.
      Terrae Sancti Pierani in Cornugallia.

207   Terra Sanctae Berrionae Virginis.
      Sancti Nietis Terra.

208 b Terra sancti Michahelis de Cornugallia.

210   Terra Comitis de Moritonio in Devenaesira.

224   Terrae Comitis de Moritonio in Cornugalliae.

234   Cornubia.

247   Cornubia.

265   Terrae Comitis de Moritonia in Summerseta.

282   Terra Comitis Eustachi in Sumerseta.

286   Terra Comitis Hugonis in Devenescira.

286 b Terra Comitis Hugonis in Summerseta.

288   Terra Balduini Vicecomitis in Devenesira.

315   Terra Balduini in Summerseta.

316   Terra Iuhelli in Devenesira.

334 b Terra Iuhelli in Corubia.

335   Terra Radulfi de Pomaria in Devenesira.

f. 344   Terra Radulfi de Pomeria in Summerseta.

345   Terra Valscini de Duaco in Devonesira.

350   Terra Walscini de Duaco in Sumerseta.

356   Terra Willelmi de Moione in Devenesira.
      Terra Willelmi de Boione in Summerseta.

366   Terra Willelmi de Falesia in Devenesira.

369   Terra Willelmi de Faleisia in Summerseta.

371   Terra Alueredi Ispaniensis in Devensira.

371 b Terra Aluredi de Hispania in Sumerseta.

376   Terra Odonis Filii Gamelini in Devenesira.

380   Terra Odonis Filii Gamelini in Summerseta.

382   Terra Torstini Filius Rofi in Devenesira.

382 b Terrae Turstini Filii Rofi in Summerseta.

386   Terra Willelmi Filius Widonis in Summerseta.
388   Terrae Goscelmi et Walteri in Devenesira.
397 b Terra Goscelmi in Cornugallia.
398   Terra Goscelmi de Essicestra.
399   Terra Willelmi Caprae in Devenesira.
407   Terra Tetbaldi Filii Bernerii in Devenesira.
411   Terra Rualdi Adobati in Devenesira.
415   Terra Willelmi de Poillei in Devenesira.
419   Terra Rotberti de Albamarla in Devenesira.
422   Terra Rogerii de Corcella in Sumerseta.
436 b Roberti Filii Geroldi in Summersete.
f. 437 Terra Edwardi Vicecomitis in Sumerseta.
438   Terra Willelmi de Ou in Sumerseta.
441   Terra Rogerii Arundelli in Sumerseta.
446   Terrae Gisleberbi Filii Turaldi in Sumerseta.
447   Terrae Osberni Gifardi in Summerseta.
447 b Terra Alueredi de Merleberga in Sumerseta.
       Terra Radulfi de Mortuomari in Sumerseta.
448 b Terra Arnulfi de Hesdinc in Sumerseta.
450   Terra Mathei de Moritanio in Summerseta.
452   Terra Serlonis de Bunceio in Summerseta.
456   Terrae Francorum Militum in Devenesira.
462 b Terrae Francorum Tegnorum in Summersete Syra.
468   Terra Nicolai Arbalestarii in Devenesira.
473 b Terra Godebaldi in Summerseta.
475   Terra Servientium Regis in Devenesira.
477   Terrae Servitium Regis in Summerseta.
481   Terrae Anglorum Tegnorum in Devensira.
490   Terrae Anglorum Tegnorum in Summersetae Syra.
495   Terrae Occupatae in Devenae Scira.
507   Terrae Occupatae in Conu Gallia.
508   Terrae Occupatae in Sumerseta.
512 b Aecclesia Sancti Petri Miceliniensis.

526   Isti sunt Hundreti de Sumerseta.

f. 527 b Total number of manors held by the church of Glastonbury in the five counties.

528 b   Total of manors held by St. Petroc in Cornwall, followed
by similar total of manors held by certain landowners
(imperfect).

532   A list of certain tenants-in-chief, beginning Dominicatus
S.REGIS.

512 b   A list of eight churches beginning with Middleton Abbey
and ending with Muchelney.

INDEX